Eugene Stefaniuk
12101 Pinehurst Place
Osoyoos, B.C. V0H 1V4
1-250-495-7708
ewhens@telus.net

Best wishes of health,
joy and peace.
may God be with you
all the days of your life,

Eugene Stefaniuk

Whose will is it?

E. Stefaniuk

WESTBOW
PRESS
A DIVISION OF THOMAS NELSON

WestBow Press books may be ordered through booksellers or by contacting:

WestBow Press
A Division of Thomas Nelson
1663 Liberty Drive
Bloomington, IN 47403
www.westbowpress.com
1-(866) 928-1240

ISBN: 978-1-4497-8367-9 (sc)

Library of Congress Control Number: 2013902082

Printed in the United States of America

WestBow Press rev. date: 2/13/2013

Did you say your prayers this morning?

Did you pray to your Heavenly Father today?

Did you ask Him that "HIS WILL (not yours) BE DONE ON EARTH AS IT IS IN HEAVEN?"

Did you get from your Heavenly Father what you asked for?

Did you thank Him for everything you have; family, food, shelter, job, car, friends, house, etc?

What happened yesterday, today, or what will happen tomorrow in your life, is not all your fault, for things that happen each and every day happen because of God's will. Many may question what this is all about. What I am trying to say is that things which happen each day in this world are happening because of God's will. You may not believe me, but all things that happen, happen because it was God's will that they happen. We seem to think that everything good that happens is from God and everything bad is from the devil. Let us look at some of the things that happened and are happening today and will happen tomorrow and see by whose will those things occur.

Was it your will or mine when, God destroyed the world with the deluge? Was it my will when more than 15,000 people perished in turkey in 1999 in an earthquake? Was it your will when again this same year in another part of the Orient hundreds of people perished in another earthquake? Whose will was it that the farmers could not harvest their crops because of bad weather? Whose will is it when thousands are hungry and die each day in Africa or other undeveloped country? Whose will was it that more than 7,000,000 Ukrainians died due to a forced starvation in 1932-33 in Ukraine? Whose will was it that Satan was allowed or permitted to bring suffering and tribulation to righteous Job?

All these things that happen each and every day around us, happen because God wills it to happen as we read in John 1:13: *"Which were born not of blood, nor of the will of the flesh, nor the will of man, but of God."* There are children born today at times with some illness and some survive and live while others die. When this happens, whose will is it which children should live and which one should die? When a plane crashes with 200 people on board, half are killed and half survive, whose will was it which ones will live and which ones will die?

Did our Lord and Savior, Who was born on this earth of the Virgin Mary do as he wanted? I do not believe so, for He himself said: *"I can of mine own self do nothing: As I hear, I judge, and My judgement is just: because I seek not Mine own will, but the will of the Father which hath sent Me." (John 5:30)* Jesus said that He cannot do anything of His own self, but the will of His and our Father. What then makes us think that what happens, happens because of our will? If Christ Himself could not do anything of His own will, what makes me/us different that we say we did it by my\our will?

When you leave on a trip or journey, do you know how it will end? Will it be safe? Will you encounter a tragedy? Will you have a misfortune thing happen on the trip? Whose will is it that our trip ends in one way or another? Apostle Paul says in the Scriptures: *"Making request, if by any means now at length I might have a prosperous journey by the Will of God to come unto you." (Romans 1:10)*

Whether by car, bus, train or plane, everyone always looks forward for a safe journey and some even put their trust in God and His will. How many people, before starting on a trip or journey seriously get down on their knees and ask God to give them a safe trip? If they did not pray for a safe trip, did they at least cross themselves as they got into the car, plane, bus? Has anyone ever boarded a plane and asked God that it crash? What we at the least can do, is cross ourselves and look forward for a safe trip to meet our loved ones at our destination. How often do we see planes crash, trains crash, buses crash, automobiles crash, and some die in those crashes, some survive. By whose will did those who died, die, and those that survived, survive? Was it your will, mine, or whose? No one else but God's will makes things happen in and around us. Everything that occurs happens by God's will.

Professions that people choose for their life, come from who? It also is the will of God. Apostle Paul's parents were bringing up their son to fit him for the rabbinical profession, but he became a man making tent-cloth from goats hair. When he was still young, he was a great adherer to the law of Moses and helped in the stoning to death of the First-Martyr, Stephen. He tortured and killed many other Christians and enjoyed in fulfilling the law he was following. But by whose will was it that this same man later became the greatest apostle of all? It was by this same God whom Paul (Saul) had his life changed around 180 degrees. On the road to Damascus when Paul was going to persecute more Christians, a change took place by whose will? To learn of his conversion from being a murderer to being the greatest apostle, read the Book of Acts 9:1-8. Paul himself tells us that he became an Apostle by the will of God: *"Paul, called to be an apostle of Jesus Christ through the will of God and Sosthenes our brother." (I Corinthians 1:1)* These same words Paul repeats in his other writings: *(II Corinthians 1:1), (Ephesians 1:1), (Colossians. 1:1), (II Timothy 1:1).* He himself says a number of times that he became an apostle by the will of God.

If a person does well to another, usually the person receiving the good, is thankful. God also rejoices when people glorify Him. A person can do well to someone, but then jealousy makes him an enemy to other people that may not have received the same

3

kind of good. How many people won large gifts and later they had enemies made, because of jealousy? By God's will, things look well and right, but people make things wrong for the Scriptures teach us: *"For so it is the will of God, that with well doing ye may put to silence the ignorance of foolish men." (I Peter 2:15)*

How many times has jealousy or greed chased someone out of their work, profession or career? Whether it is in church or civil life, we find this happening day in and day out in today's time. Power hungry, greedy and jealous people have hurt many others and taken away livelihoods of others. We can take for an example a person that served the Lord, but then cannot serve anymore because someone else may have wanted to show and use their power and authority. Apostle Peter says: *"For it is better if the will of God be so, that ye suffer for well doing, then for evil doing."(I Peter 3:17)* How many servants of God did nothing wrong and evil, did not steal or murder, but were "well doing," but now they cannot serve the Lord any more at the altar. Apostle Peter continues to tell us: *"Wherefore let them that suffer according to the will of God commit the keeping of their souls to Him in well doing, as unto a faithful Creator." (I Peter 4:19)* Those that have done well unto God, always will continue doing well in other ways and be in peace with God. David writes in his Psalms: *"I delight to do the will, O my God: yea Thy law is within my heart. I have preached righteousness in the great congregation: low I have not refrained my lips, O Lord, Thou knows." (Psalm 40:8-9)*

The best lesson or knowledge to learn of life in the world, is the story of Job. As we read his story, we see he was a righteous, kind, obedient and good man, yet, why did he have to suffer so much grief, pain and agony? Whose will was it that he went through so much disaster in his life? Could God not have stopped him from going through "hell" on earth? It was God's will that Job suffered so much tribulation. Did Satan take over Job's life because Job was not God-loving or God-fearing? Every day Job prayed, thanked and glorified God. He was a just man, but God permitted (willed?) that Satan do as he pleased with Job, but at the same time Satan could not touch Job's soul. God willed that Satan can use his power to try and destroy Job if he can and succumb Job to Satan, but Job stood steadfast in his faith in God, and in the end God rewarded Job with even greater love, faith, wealth and goodness that he previously had possessed. One may read the whole story of Job from the Book of Job in the Bible.

There are other examples in the Holy Scripture about things that happened to people, because it was God's will. Let us look at another of God's righteous people - Abraham. His story is found in the Holy Scripture in the first book of Moses or as it is called Genesis. Let us look only at one part of Abraham's life in the Book of Genesis 22:1-13. What had Abraham's son Isaac done wrong, or even Abraham himself, that God instructed Abraham to kill his own son Isaac as a sacrifice? Whose will was it that Abraham go to the mountain and kill his own son? God was testing and trying out by His will how strong Abraham's faith was in God. God wanted to know if Abraham would be obedient to Him. God seeing Abraham's love to Him, then prevents the killing of Isaac. Yet it was God's will telling Abraham that He wanted Abraham to kill his son and again it was God's will that he does not kill his son at the last moment. God's will put a ram with locked horns in the brush for a sacrifice. God always wants our love, like the parents want their children's love toward them. When you give someone something, you expect to get thanks and appreciation for it. When God gives us health, food, families, sunshine, rain, jobs etc., are we thankful to God for all these things? God's will is that we also give thanks to Him for everything like apostle Paul says: *"In everything give thanks: for this is the will of God in Christ Jesus concerning you."* (I Thessalonians 5:18) Have you been thanking God for all that you have, for all that He has given you? It is God's will that He be thanked as apostle Paul says to do.

How many people do you know that make donations, try to help others, try to do good, yet many of such people do things because all they want is to get glory from others around them. They want to be praised and glorified for what they did. People of this type, God spoke about as we read in the Scriptures: *"For as much as their lips do honour Me, but they removed their hearts far from me."(Isaiah 29:13)* Where is your heart? Where is your neighbours' heart? Where is your friend's heart according to God? Where is your family's heart? God knows where your heart is because Christ Himself said: *"For where your treasure is, there will your heart be also."* (Matthew 6:21) So what is your treasure...a new house, high salary, holidays, family, a new truck....?

In our lives today we see people who are religious and are trying to please God, but not willingly, because they want to seek out for themselves fame, fortune and glory. They want people to see what they did, what they gave, so that their names are proclaimed for all to see and know. All that is wrong, because instead of being humble and faithful they only want glory for themselves. Apostle Peter says: *"Not with eye service, as men pleasers; but as servants of Christ, doing the will of God from the heart, with good will doing service, as to the Lord, and not to men; knowing that whatsoever good thing any man does, the same shall receive of the Lord whether he be bond or free."* *(Ephesians 6:6-8)* So when you give or do things, do it with a free heart for *"God loves a cheerful giver."* *(II Corinthians 9:7)*.

Then we have another story or historical fact from the Bible about Zacharias and Elizabeth. By whose will did those things happen in their life as they happened? The Bible says: *"They were both righteous before God, walking in all commandments and ordinances of the Lord blameless."(Luke 1:6)* Here we see a perfect couple as the Scriptures tells us. They loved God, thanked Him, did things by His will and as we could say were "very good church goers." Yet there was one thing lacking in their life. The Bible says:

"And they had no children, because that Elizabeth was barren, and they both were now well stricken in years." (Luke 1:7) They were a childless couple well advanced in their years, and Elizabeth past the childbearing age. We know that Zacharias could not speak for some nine months until the birth of their son, John the Baptist. We say that this is a miraculous story because an old woman gives birth to a child. By whose will, was this miraculous act done to this righteous family? They were God-loving and lived a God-fearing life, but what happened to them was it not only by the will of God? By whose will was Elizabeth barren until she gave birth to John the Baptist in her late years?

The story about the man being born blind. We cannot realize this happening to a person, being born blind at birth and so we immediately would ask a question, why? This true story happened because it was God's will to be so. The Apostles were eager and wanted to know by whose sin the man was born blind, by his sin or the sins of his parents. Jesus replied that neither sinned:"*Neither hath this man sinned nor his parents: but that the works of God should be made manifest in him.*" *(John 9:3)* Again we see here that God's will was that this man be born blind. Today, surgeons would probably try to perform some surgery for such a person and again whether it would work would depend upon God's will. Yet in this instance Jesus made mud with his spit, put the mud on the man's blind eyes (no surgery) and told the man to go wash his eyes in the pool of Siloam. He did as was told, and for the first time in his life he could see, his eyes were opened. Again this event shows us that it was God's will for all this that happened.

What about Simeon in the temple? When Jesus was forty days old, He was brought to the temple for the purification of His Mother, the Virgin Mary. Jesus was brought to the temple and Simeon's eyes saw what no one else could see. Upon seeing Jesus who He was, Simeon said: "*Lord, now let thy servant depart in peace, according to the word: For mine eyes have seen the salvation.*" *(Luke 2:29-30)* Simeon had been foretold that he would not die until he saw Christ Jesus. He could see who Christ was when Jesus was brought to the temple and we ask, by whose will, had all this been done? Again I say, that all things that happen, happen by God's will.

Another fine example we could look at is, is the story of Noah. Everyone knows about Noah, his life and family. We all know that it was Noah, his wife, their three sons and their wives who were the only ones that were saved on the face of the earth from the flood. Along with them a pair of all living creatures on earth were also saved in the ark. So we ask,- by whose will was the world destroyed? Was it Noah's will? Was it the will of his wife? Was it their son's will? God never meant to destroy this earth, but because of the corruption on it, it was His will that He destroy everything and then start clean again with new life on earth after the deluge. It was by His will that everything on earth was destroyed.

We can look at another episode that is recorded in the Holy Scriptures. Most of us have heard the story of Samson from the Old Testament. We know how Samson killed a thousand men with a jawbone. We know how he killed a lion with nothing more then his own bare hands. We know by whose will he received his power and strength. We know of the suffering that Samson received from the hands of the philistines and how they took out his eyes. We also know how Samson lost his strength, betrayed by the woman - Delilah. When he told his secret in what lay his strength, his hair was cut and he was like any other ordinary person, with the same strength. In the end we know how his strength returned, how he pushed the pillars of the building apart with his strength and three thousand people died. All this and the story and life of Samson was done by God's will. *(Judges chapters 13-16)*

What about the Annunciation to the Virgin Mary by an Angel sent from God to tell Her that She will bare the Son of God. By whose will did the Angel come to tell Mary the news? And after this news was proclaimed by the Angel, Christ was born by whose will? Was He born by Herod's will? Joseph and Mary had to flee from the hands of Herod. Again they were warned by an Angel to leave their land and flee to Egypt.

All this was by the will of God. After Christ was crucified, we again can ask, by whose will was He crucified, by Pilate's will? Pilate didn't want to hurt Jesus because he said: *"Why, what evil hath He done?" (Matthew 27:23)* We also read in Luke thus: *"Ye have brought this Man unto me, as one that perverts the people: and behold I, having examined Him before you, have found no fault in this man touching those things whereof ye accuse Him." (Luke 23:14)* Was it not Christ's will that He die for us for our sins? It was not the will of Herod or Pilate, but Jesus's(God) own will that He died for the sins of this world.

Then what about John the Baptist? He is the Baptizer of Jesus. He lost his life by whose will? By Herod and Herodias? Do you think that God could not have prevented the beheading of John the Baptist? To us things are impossible, but God can do anything and everything, for even the Scriptures tell us:*"With men this is impossible; but with God all things are possible." (Matthew 19:26).* God could have prevented the beheading of John the Baptist, but His will was that it should happen as it did. Did John the Baptist do something wrong that he had to lose his life in such horrific manner - beheading?

We say that all bad things happen because of Satan or the devil twisting our mind and making us follow him. Can God not stop the devil from doing evils which we have on earth today? Could God not have stopped the devil from causing all the grief to Job? If He could have stopped that, could He not stop everything else bad that is happening on earth today? All things that happen good, or bad, happen because God permits them to happen by His will. The bad happens, so that people would learn from it and become sons and daughters of God instead children of the devil.

Another example of God's will is shown with Daniel. Daniel was thrown into the hungry Lions' den. Why did the lions not devour Daniel? Was it Daniels will, or the will of the lions that he was not killed? Were the lions not hungry? Were the lions afraid of Daniel? Did Daniel tell them not to devour him? Then what about Daniels three friends, Shadrach, Meshach and Abednego? They were cast into a fiery furnace which was heated up seven times normal then usual. Yet, the three of them were not consumed by the fire. Why not? By whose will? The Scriptures say: *"Upon whose bodies the fire had no power, nor was a hair of their head singed, neither were their coats changed, nor the smell of fire passed on them."* *(Daniel 3:27)* By whose will did all this take place with Daniel and his three friends? Was it not by the will of God?

In another place we find David and God's will being fulfilled again. David had two wives, but he once saw another beautiful woman, Bathsheba and committed a sin with her. Bathsheba's husband Uriah was away at war. David got Joab to see that Uriah was killed, so he put him in the front battle lines. When news reached David that Uriah was dead, David then married Bathsheba. His sin was great, adultery and murder. David's punishment should have been death, because this was against God's Commandments. But God by His will, sent a prophet Nathan to visit David. David having listened to Nathan, confessed his sin for having Uriah killed. God forgave David his sin as the Scripture says: *"And David said unto the Nathan, I have sinned against the Lord. And Nathan said unto David.. The Lord hath put away thy sin: thou shalt not die." (II Samuel 12:13)* By whose will did all this happen with David the king? God could have prevented and stopped all the things from happening in the first place. God causes for things that happened and are happening today. And in the end He Who forgave David his sins, forgives ours today when we abide by his Commandments?

We are all God's children whether we think so or not. In our daily lives we try to do things as we may wish or by our will, but many, many times those things do not get fulfilled the way we planned. Why? Because it was not God's will that it be done that is why. My late mother said many times, "People make plans and God changes them." Jesus said that we can't do anything without Him: *"I am the vine, ye are the branches: he that abides in Me, and*

I in him, the same brings forth much fruit: For without Me, ye can do nothing." (John 15:5) How true.

By those words it must mean that anything we do is done with His will, for He says that without Him we can't do anything. Without God a person can do nothing, no matter how hard one may try. If you have enough faith and believe in God, you will even be able to move mountains, but only with God's help and will. If you wanted to move a mountain into the deepest part of an ocean, it could be done only with strong faith and more so with God's will. To see how true this is we look into the Bible and find how Peter was fishing all night and caught not a fish. Christ came along and told him to throw the net in the deep part of the water. Momentarily he caught so much fish that his boat was beginning to sink and he called on his friends to come and give him a hand. Read this story in the Bible in Luke 5:1-11. By whose will was this done?

In the Old Testament we find another episode of God's will, the destruction of Sodom and Gomorrah. My understanding of this tells me that it was God's will in destroying the two cities. When Lot's wife turned back to see the destruction, she was turned into a pillar of salt. God's will was that she not turn to look back at what was happening to the two cities. Whose will was it that told Lot to leave the two cities with his family? Lot and his daughter were also saved by God's will. Was it Lot's will or his wife's to destroy the two cities? If not Lot's will, than whose?

Another historical fact is the story of Moses. By whose will was Moses saved, when other children were being put to death? God's will prevented Moses from being killed, because God had other plans for Moses. God could have had Moses killed like other small children, but that was not God's will to happen. After Moses escaped with his life from Egypt, God met him on the mountain and told him to go back to Egypt to save God's people. Moses was afraid and not sure if he should go back to Egypt and he tried in vain to free himself from not going back, because he was sure that he would meet death there. The Bible tells us: *"And Moses said to God; who am I, that I should go unto pharaoh, and that I should bring forth the children of Israel out of Egypt?" (Exodus 3:11)* But God's will was that He would make and have Moses go to Egypt for God told Moses: *"Certainly I will be with thee."(Exodus 3:12).*

God told Moses in advance that the pharaoh will not want to let His people go: *"And I am sure that the king of Egypt will not let you go, no not by a mighty hand."(Exodus 3:19)* Moses still was not convinced that he should and will go. God's will was that Moses must go but Moses kept insisting not to go and says; *"But behold, they will not believe nor hearken unto my voice." (Exodus 4:1)* All this time God is convincing Moses to go and then Moses again says: *"O, my Lord. I am not eloquent, neither theretofore, nor since Thou hast spoken unto thy servant: but I am slow of speech, and of a slow tongue." (Exodus 4:11)* All this time Moses was trying to tell God that he can't do what God wants him to do and this made God angry:*"And the anger of the Lord was kindled against Moses." (Exodus 4:14)*

Finally when Moses could no longer stand up to God, he did as God's will was and went to Egypt. God knew by His will that the pharaoh would not let God's people go: *"And the Lord said unto Moses; when thou goest to return into Egypt, see that thou do all those wonders before pharaoh, which I have put into thine hand: but I will harden his heart, that he shall not let the people go." (Exodus 4:21)* By whose will, was the pharaoh's heart hardened? God told Moses to go set His people free, but God would harden pharaohs' heart not to let the people go. Was it Moses's will that pharaoh's heart was hardened? Was it Aaron's will? All that happened, did so by God's will. After Moses led God's people out of Egypt, why did it take forty years to move across the few hundred miles; *"Unto*

a good land and large, unto a land flowing with milk and honey."
(Exodus 3:38) When Moses went to Egypt, ten different plagues
had to be inflicted upon pharaoh and his people before he let the
Hebrews go. By whose will were the plagues created upon the
Egyptians? The whole action and of the life of Moses in the Bible
was all done by the will of God.

Another Old Testament story about Joseph and his brothers.
Joseph was hated by his brothers. They had put him into a well
where there was no water, but later took him out and sold him
to merchants for twenty pieces of silver, *(Genesis 37:28)* To make
the long story short, in the end Joseph was the hero when his
brothers came to buy food from the country where Joseph was
living. All this happened by the will of God. God wanted it to be
that way, and that way it was. The same happens today, by God's
will, whether good or bad. By whose will are earthquakes caused?
By whose will do hurricanes kill people and cause damage? By
whose will is it that there is drought in the world and thousands
of people die of hunger each year?

In the Holy Scriptures we read of many miracles that
happened in both the Old and the New Testaments. One such
miracle in the New Testament is the feeding of more than five
thousand people with five loaves of bread and two fishes. We say
that it was a miracle that so many people could be fed with so
few supplies of food. The miracle was the will of God that such
a feat was performed. We also read of the blind man having his
eyesight restored, and the water turned into wine, the healing of
the hemorrhaging woman and other miracles and the greatest one
of all, Christ's Resurrection. We ask ourselves, by whose will did
all these miracles occur?

Clergy serve the Divine Liturgy every Sunday. During a
certain time in the Liturgy, the Holy Spirit (unseen), comes down
upon the gifts on the altar and transforms them into the Body
and Blood of Christ. By whose will does this transformation take

place? Is it the will of the priest, the faithful at the service, or is it due to the will of God? By the will of God, the priest can perform each and every service. If God willed that the priest not serve, it would be that way, but God's will is that the Liturgy be served. Even by the will of God, people attend the services. Everything that happens on earth each and every day happens because of God's will that it happen.

We saw, heard and still see and hear of wars around the world each and every day. We say that war is the work of the devil. It may be done by the devil, but by God's will. Just as the devil was causing Job all his tribulation, yet he was doing it by God permitting the devil to do so. Could God not have told the devil that Job cannot be tortured and it would have been thus? Could God have not stopped all the evil against Job at any time? When we mention war, what about the war on the small infants and children two years and younger that were killed on Herod's instructions to destroy the children? Could God not have prevented 14,000 small innocent and guiltless children from being slaughtered? What wrong did the small children do that they had to be destroyed so savagely? Was it by their wills that they died? Was it by the will of their parents? Those little children were the first martyrs for Christ. They gave their life for Christ even before First-martyr Stephen did.

Look around you today. Look at all the technological world around you. We say that man has invented all of this technology around us: electricity, telephones, freezers, televisions, air-conditioning, computers, satellites and thousands of other inventions. Maybe some are good, some maybe are bad like the bombs, herbicides and the pesticides, etc. By whose will have all these things been invented? Why were they not invented two thousand or one thousand years ago, but now during our age and times? Could God have not prevented all these inventions from being invented and discovered? By whose will did man reach such a high wisdom?

In the Bible we also read of Jairus' daughter being resurrected from the dead. Lazarus was also resurrected from the dead after being four days in the tomb. Then there was also the resurrection of a widow's son in the little village of Nain. Christ's Resurrection is the greatest of all miracles. By whose will did those resurrections take place? By whose will did Lazarus walk out of the grave after you could smell his body wasting away? *"Martha the sister of him that was dead, saith unto Him, Lord by this time he stinks: for he hath been dead four days." (John 11:39)* Jesus had come to the grave of Lazarus and did what? *"And Jesus lifted up His eyes, and said, Father, I thank Thee that Thou hast heard Me." (John 11:41)* So by whose will did Lazarus resurrect? By whose will did the dead resurrect and walk the streets when Christ was Crucified? *"And the graves were opened; and many bodies of the saints, which slept arose, and came out of the graves after His Resurrection, and went into the holy city and appeared unto many." (Matthew 27:52-53)*

What about the story of Jericho? Even a song has been written that the "Walls of Jericho came tumbling down." How many times have we read or heard about the miraculous way how the walls fell down around Jericho? God had told Joshua how he would take the city of Jericho. And Joshua did not need bulldozers to knock down the city walls. For six days the people quietly marched around Jericho making no noise. On the seventh day they marched seven times around and shouted. What happened? The walls of Jericho fell to the ground. By whose will? Read about this miracle in the Book of Joshua 6:1-20.

In today's materialistic world people are doing as they please, and it is by my understanding that they do these things by God's will. He gave us a free will, and if so why then can we not get what we want? Why are there many religious, church going, God loving and God-fearing people that have so many problems? Why does a clergyman's son have to be shot in school? Did this young lad's father, a preacher, teach people to steal, rob, assault or kill? What is the reason that many God-loving people go through much suffering and by whose will? They pray, they go to church, they help the poor, they donate when and wherever is needed, they teach their children right from wrong, they are righteous and still they suffer and go through grief, heartache and pain. By whose will, then does that harm come to them? Is it not the same as Job was, a righteous man and still by the will of God he suffered such grief and pain?

Many people do as they please, sinning against God and they say that God is merciful will not punish His children (us). They say that Christ died on the cross for our sins and we don't have to worry any more for God will not punish us. But what does God say about punishment? We find in the Scriptures a number of places that God will punish us up to the third and fourth generation for our sins. Today we see in this world floods, tornadoes, hurricanes, mud slides, earthquakes, avalanches and other disasters around us and we say it is "nature's havoc" or "mother nature." But then, what is mother nature?

All these tribulations that are befalling us is nothing more than God's punishments for our sins or sins of our parents, grand parents or great grandparents. What will happen to the third or fourth generation down the road in your family for your sins you are committing today? We don't know what kind of punishments God has in store for us or our future generations for our sins that we are doing today. God very plainly says that He will punish us, even though He is a loving God. We read: *"Keeping mercy for thousands, forgiving iniquity and transgression and sin, and that will by no means clear the guilty: visiting the iniquities of the fathers upon the children, and upon the children's children, unto the third and to the fourth generation." (Exodus 34:7)* and *(Numbers 14:18)* God is long-suffering and merciful, but if people do not want to repent and change their ways of life, God's will is that He is left with no choice but to send down upon us His punishments as far as the third and fourth generation.

Some people will not pay heed and attention to these words of God. They will turn around defend their sinful ways and say: "But that was in the Old Testament and we are living in a new world and Christ died for our sins and we don't follow the old laws." But Jesus Himself in the New Testament says: *"Think not that I come to destroy the law, or the prophets: I come not to destroy, but to fulfil."* (*Matthew 5:17*)

It could also be said that God punishes us because He loves us. We read in Hebrews 12:6 thus: *"For whom the Lord loves He chastens and scourges every son who He receives."* He is like a good parent in the home. When a child does something wrong or disobedient, the child will get punished, not that the parent hates that child, but to teach it right from wrong. From time to time God by His will punishes us, for we are His children and as the Scripture says: *"He that spares his rod, hates his son; but he that loves him chastens him betimes."* (*Proverbs 13:24*) Reading in "The New Bible Commentary" by the Rev. Professor F. Davidson M.A., D.D. and assistants, Rev. A.M. Stibbs M.A. and Rev. E. F. Kevan M. Th., we read on page 1110, that God allows for trials and misfortunes to come upon the people and that He makes people endure such griefs and trials.

Even in the New Testament we find repetition of what God said in the Old Testament. We read in Hebrews 12:6-13 the following: *"For whom the Lord loves, He chastens, and scourges every son whom He receives. If we endure chastening, God deals with you as with sons; for what son is he whom the father chastens not? But if ye be without chastisement, whereof all are partakers, then are ye bastards, and not sons. Furthermore we have had fathers of our flesh which corrected us, and we gave them reverence: shall we not much rather be in subjection unto the Father of spirits, and live? For they verily for a few days chastened us after their own pleasure; but He for our profit, that we might be partakers of His holiness. Now no chastening for the present seems to be joyous, but grievous: nevertheless after ward it yields the peaceful fruit of the righteousness unto them which are exercised thereby."*

On October 11, 1999 at the 11:00 P.M. CTV news read by Sandi Renaldo, a news item read that a highway tragedy occurred in Saskatchewan. A family was going to church to a Thanksgiving service. A father, mother and three teenage children died in the crash. The accident occurred near Norquay, Sask. By whose will did this tragedy take place that the whole family was wiped out? The family was going to church to pray, going to give thanks to God. They were not going to a hotel or bar to get drunk and have a good time. They were not going to some sports spectacle. They were not going to rob someone or to cause vandalism. They were a God loving people on the way to church to pray and thank God.

Does God not want people to be grateful to Him, to thank Him for everything that we have? If the devil caused this crash and elimination of the family, how could he do that without God's will? When the devil tempted Job, God told him that he could do as he pleased with Job, but he could not touch Job's soul. The devil has no right to a person's soul. The soul belongs to God and God can do as He pleases with it. It is God's will whether we live or die, how and when we die. So who gave the devil the permission to take the souls of five innocent people? If the accident happened by the devil's work, still God had to give the devil permission to eliminate those five lives. The devil did not touch Job's soul.

We all heard of the story of the ten lepers which Christ healed. One of them came back to thank Christ and nine did not. By whose will were the ten lepers healed? By whose will did one come back to thank Christ? By God's will. This happened so that Jesus could use that as an example to teach us how ungrateful we are to God for His mercies, goodness and blessings upon us. One leper came back and thanked Christ for God's great mercy. Ten percent thanked the Lord for making him well. The other nine lepers or 90% did not thank God for being healed. We can look at ourselves today and ask ourselves to which group do we belong? To the 10% group or the 90% group. Do you thank God for everything you get, or do you not have time to thank God? Can you not find 2-3 minutes each morning and night to thank God for everything you receive from Him? Do you thank Him for the food you eat? Do you thank Him for everything you have in your home? Do you thank Him for your family? Do you thank Him for your health? The story of people's ungratefulness to God can be read in Luke 17:11-19, the story about of the ten lepers.

I have already mentioned about resurrection of the dead by Christ. But another incident that happened was the raising of the widow's son who had died. A poor widow had been living with her son and her only hope. She looked forward when one day she would die and her son would bury her. But God's will was different. The young man died and the poor widow was left alone with no one to turn to except the people that followed the funeral procession. She was a widow. Who will look after her now that her son is dead?

As the body was carried out of the village of Nain, Jesus stopped the procession because as the Bible says: *"He had compassion on her and said unto her, weep not."(Luke 7:13)* Christ stopped the bier and told the young man: *"Arise."* The Bible says that after this happened: *"there came a fear on all."* *(Luke 7:16)* People had never heard of such a thing, not alone to see a dead person resurrect and come back to life. All happened by God's will. This event ends happily and the Bible says: *"And they glorified God, saying, that a great prophet is risen among us; and that God hath visited His people."* *(Luke 17:16)* The widow and the people were thankful to God, *"And they glorified God"* for having raised her son from the dead. How many people gather in church on Sunday to thank God for everything they have? There are two groups of people on this earth, those that thank God and those that don't. A good time would be to stop and think when Thanksgiving comes. Do we thank God for your things you have or you don't even think about it.

Another event in the Bible we see is when Christ came to the pool of Bethesda in Jerusalem. There He found many people waiting to be healed. The Bible says: *"For an angel went down at a certain season into the pool, and troubled the waters."* *(John 5:4)* The angel came down and troubled the waters by whose will? Farther on we read of Christ having a conversation with a man who had been a paralytic for some 38 years of his life. God is an all-knowing God. He knows everything because the Bible says: *"When Jesus saw him lying, and knew that he had been now a long time in that case."* *(John 5:6)*

Jesus knew that the man had been in that position (paralytic) for a long time. When Jesus saw the sick man, He asked him if he wanted to be well. Now who does not want to be well, healthy and strong? When the Angel stirred the water the first person to go into the pool after the stirring of the water that person would be well no matter what illness they may have had. (John 5:4) Yet the man that had been a paralytic for 38 years did not go into the pool, for Jesus says to him: *"Rise, take up thy bed, and walk."* *(John 5:8)* By whose will was the man made well? Was it by the will of the Angel that troubled the water? Was it by some other person by the pool? It was God's will that the man be made well so that people could see and learn about Jesus. Another very important thing about this healed man is what Jesus told him later in the temple. *"After ward Jesus finds him in the temple, and said unto him, Behold, thou art made whole: sin no more lest a worse thing come unto you."* *(John 5:14)* The man had been ill for 38 years (John 5:5). Can you imagine yourself spending half of your life in a paralytic way? What worse could come to a person, yet Jesus says: *"lest a worse thing come unto thee."* *(John 5:14)* Jesus warned the man as He warns us today: *"Sin no more....."* Check yourself, and see if you abide by God's law, or did you make your own laws?

One day as Jesus was together with His apostles, He told them of what they can expect in their life in the world they were living in. He said that they would be persecuted, scourged, testified against, etc. (Matthew 10:17-18). He kept telling them what would happen in this ruthless world. He said: *"Brother shall deliver brother to death and the father the child and the children shall rise up against their parents and cause them to put to death."* *(Matthew 10:21)* But that was not all that Christ knew would happen and what more He had to tell the Apostles. He continued: *"And ye shall be hated of all men."* *(Matthew 10:22)* Then He told them what they must do: *"But when they persecute you in the city, flee ye unto another."* *(Matthew 10:23)*

Then the next thing Christ told His Apostles is very important in today's times. It is prevalent in our country every day and especially so in the last three or four decades if not more. Each time we turn on the news we hear of people going on strike against their company, government, boss, etc. Jesus knew this would happen and He said: *"The disciple is not above his master, nor the servant above his lord."(Matthew 10:24)* In today's world the workers have revolted against their masters who hired them and gave them a job. The workers keep telling their master (boss) what he has to do. Yet Jesus very plainly said that the worker is not above his lord (boss). The workers keep telling the boss how much pay they have to receive, how many hours a day they must work, how many times a day they have to stop for coffee breaks, how much holiday time they must have, what kind of working conditions they need, etc.

When we see the workers striking against their company or their lord, is it a wonder that we hear people saying: "What is this world coming to anyway?" It is coming to destruction because of the disobedience of the labour or work force against their boss or company. They keep demanding more and more and more each time and no one knows when it will stop and when it will be enough.

The people that are on strike don't think about someone else that may not have a job. They don't want to share their income. They think only of themselves to get as much as they can and that is called greed. When a worker gets $20.00 an hour today and says it is not enough then something must be wrong. How many old people are there that live alone and live only on their old age monthly pay check and they say they are getting by. They get an old age pension check which gives them about $30.00 per day, if that. The worker gets that and some even more in an hour. The poor old aged people say it's enough, the younger one says it's not enough. How much is enough?

When you have a new modern home, 2-4 vehicles in the driveway, a motor home, boats, skido, and every other thing they can think of in your home, and then turn around and say you have to work less and get paid more. For what? There used to be a saying: "No work, no pay." The Holy Scripture says: *"For even when we were with you, this we commanded you, that if any would not work, neither should he eat." (II Thessalonians 3:10)* The Bible is clear that if you don't work, you should not eat. When the strikers are out on strike they are not working, but do they not eat? We also see the workers demands are getting greater each time. People used to work six days a week. Finally the workers reached the point where they worked five days a week. Now in many places people work only four days a week. What did God say about working? In the Bible we read: *"Remember the Sabbath, to keep it holy. Six days shalt thou labour, and do all thy work: but the seventh day is the Sabbath of the Lord thy God; in it thou shalt not do any work, thou, thy son nor thy daughter, nor thy manservant, nor thy maidservant, nor thy cattle, nor thy stranger that is within thy gates. For in six days the Lord made heaven and earth, the sea, and all that in them is, and rested the seventh day; wherefore the Lord blessed the Sabbath day and hallowed it." (Exodus 20: 8-11).*

People have broken and are still breaking God's commandments. People don't even know what the Sabbath is anymore. They work day in and day out and never seem to get richer - and they never will. God's will was and is that people work six days a week and the Sabbath day to rest, to go to church and thank God for everything. But instead of going to church, people head to sports spectacles, fishing, golfing, hunting, lawn work, shopping, etc. Is that what the Bible tells us to do on the Sabbath? Then we wonder why this world is turning upside down and nothing seems to be going right. Stop, repent, change and follow God's way if you want and wish for things to be even better than they are now.

Are people short of clothing, food, shelter etc., that they have to go on strike to get a higher wage? I have yet to see someone who has starved or who is walking around naked in Canada because their wage is to low. If they haven't got clothes or food, what about the people in Kosovo, in Africa, Serbia, Mexico, South America and other third world countries? Do they have better clothing and more food than we have? Do they have better homes than we have? Do they get a higher wage than we do? Do they have better appliances than we do? Why are we complaining so much about being off so bad in comparison to the third world countries? You should be happy that you have all you have, and be thankful to God for it.

If life in our country is so bad, then maybe the complainers should quit their jobs, leave this country and go to one of the third world countries and they will be satisfied there. No one is forcing them to suffer so much that they own 2-4 vehicles, modern homes, all kinds of gadgets, etc., Why don't we look into the Holy Book and follow the rules for living from it? Then we won't have to worry and say; "What is this world coming to?" Look into the Bible and read the story of Lazarus and the rich man. It is found in Luke 16:19-31.Everyone should read this story and put themselves in the place of Lazarus or the rich man. Learn from this story what reward you may expect from God from your way of life and your demands that at times are outrageous. Ask yourself, by whose will are you well off, compared to the people in other countries of the world? Is it not God's will?

All things that happen, happen because of God's will. Yes by God's will. It is true that God gave us a will to choose between right and wrong, but can't God prevent us from doing wrong at anytime He wishes? Look at the Fifth Sunday of fast (lent) each year as we celebrate and commemorate St. Mary of Egypt. We know what kind of a life she lived and in a promiscuous way.

One day when she travelled to the Holy Land, she saw many people going to a church. She wanted to go in with them with the thought she would find more companions to share in her ways of life. As the story says, people were going into the church, yet when she tried to go in she could not. Some unforeseen power held her back. She tried and tried to walk in but something held her back. She looked at her friends and they all looked as a wretched group of people. She turned around and ran out of the church yard and no one ever saw her again until a year before her death when a monk found her in the wilderness and gave her Holy Communion a few days before Easter. She had spent four decades in the wilderness. Every year she is remembered not for her promiscuous life, but for her repentance and prayer. In the wilderness she had nothing. She did not have a modern home. She did not have the food and clothing like we have today. Today she has something that many probably will not have, and that is eternal life in heaven. By whose will did Mary of Egypt's life turn around? Was it her will? Was it her friend's will? It was God's will like it is with everything else. We can look at another example that God's will, will always be His way. Look at Apostle Paul. He was one the greater persecutors of Christians in his time as he himself testifies in many of his writings. He persecuted, murdered and tortured Christians and Christ's church. It was God's will that Apostle Paul be changed and became the greatest Apostle and a Christian. We can read in the Book of Acts about Paul's work against the Christians, God's church and how he was converted into a Christian on the road to Damascus. *(Acts 9: 1-9)* By whose will did Paul's conversion take place?

Later Paul tells us in his writing to the Corinthians how he escaped death. The governor in Damascus kept a garrison to watch Paul, but Paul was let down in a basket to safety. *(II Corinthians 11:32-33)* By whose will did Paul escape from the governor? There was also an impending death for Apostle Peter as we read in *(Acts 12:1-9*. Again we can ask ourselves: by whose will was Peter saved?

A similar thing happened to Paul and Silas. Death was staring Paul in his teeth, but God's will was that Paul not die at that moment because God had other plans for him and there was work to be done. First Paul and Silas were beaten nearly to death and then thrown into the prison and a guard posted to watch over them. At midnight a miracle happened (by God's will), when an earthquake shook so hard: *"that the foundations of the prison were shaken and immediately all the doors were opened and everyone's bands were loosed."* (Acts 16:26)

When all this happened the guard was sure that the prisoners had escaped and he was going to run his sword into himself. Paul seeing what was about to happen cried out: *"Do thyself no harm: for we are all here."* (Acts 16:27-28) Next morning during daylight the magistrate learning about what happened over night sent an order saying: *"Let those men go."* (Acts 16: 35-36) By whose will did all this happen and take place? Only God can do these things as He can do everything else because to God nothing is impossible. Even the hairs on your head will not fall off your head by the will of God. One bird will not fall out of the sky by God's will. *(Matthew 10:29-30)* As "The Orthodox Study Bible" says on page 30: *"God takes care of sparrows (Matthew 10:29, 31) and the hairs of your head (10:30) are numbered, then He has the power of creating, sustaining, and providing for everything, even to the smallest detail."*

Every day that we live, we see so many people being concerned with trivial things in their lives. They create canons, rules, laws, by-laws, regulations, etc., to give themselves power to rule over others. Laws that were set up 100, 500, 1500 years ago and more have not been changed and the leaders, churches, organizations abide by some laws and look through their fingers at others. There is a saying: "Laws are made to be broken." It was also God's will that Apostle James wrote: *"For whosoever shall keep the whole law, and yet offend in one point, he is guilty of all."(James 2:10)* Therefore no one can ever say or think that they are perfect and someone else is a sinner, for if you even break one little law, you are as guilty as anyone else.

Is it not what one's heart says or shows what the person is? Apostle Paul also wrote to the Romans mentioning twice that no one is perfect for he says: *"For all have sinned, and come short of the glory of God." (Romans 3:23)* and also *"Wherefore, as by one man sin entered into the world, and death by sin: and so death passed upon all men, for that all have sinned." (Romans 5:12).* So let no one think that he or she is better then the next person for each and everyone living and walking on the face of this earth is a sinner.

God's will does everything on earth and around us. Go to the hospital or better yet, go to a nursing home. Look around at the patients who can't even feed themselves, who haven't taken a step in years because they are in a wheelchair. Look at the ones that can't speak or say a word. Look at the one that has been bedridden for years and is staring at space and can't even recognize his own family members. By whose will do these people go through that "hell on earth?" By whose will did Job go through the same kind of suffering? Who gave permission for the devil to do as he pleased with Job, but couldn't touch his soul? Was it not God who permitted the devil the freedom to do with Job as he wished?

Previously I have mentioned that even Jesus can do nothing by Himself, but as His Father wills it. In John we read: *"Then said Jesus unto them, when ye have lifted the Son of man, then shall ye know that I am He, and that I do nothing of Myself: but as My Father hath taught Me, I speak these things." (John 8:28)* If Jesus can't do things by Himself, why do we sinners and weaklings put into our minds that we can do everything without God? If we be so wise, then let us prevent the earthquakes, hurricanes, diseases, death, tornadoes, etc. We can't prevent those things because they are all caused by the will of God to happen. Jesus said: *"I can of Myself do nothing. As I hear, I judge; and My judgement is righteous, because I do not seek My own will, but the will of the Father who sent Me."(John 5:30)* Even Jesus did the will of His Father.

I remember one Romanian man in Calgary telling me a true story about a young Romanian lad who had immigrated to Canada, learned English and got a job with an oil company. His parents were back in Romania. This young lad drove a truck for the oil company and while driving one day he was involved in a roll over accident. He was unconscious and in a coma when he was brought to a hospital. The doctors tried to save his life but there was nothing they could do, and he was put on life support. There was no hope for him. In order to remove the life supports they needed a family member to sign papers. They got hold of the family in Romania, told them what happened, and that there was no hope for their son.

They asked that someone come to Canada to sign papers to take their son or brother of the life support. The family decided the mother would go because she wanted to see her son for the last time before he dies. With an aching and grieving heart, the mother boards a plane and heads to Canada. After a short flight, something goes wrong with the plane, the plane crashes and the mother is killed. Some time later the young man in the hospital began to come around. Slowly he recovered, became well and was back at his old job working for the same oil company. Now we can ask ourselves, by whose will did all these things happen? Who permitted this to occur as it did? God permits evil to happen to people as He also blesses people with good things. By whose will did the plane crash? By whose will did the young man recover when the doctors said that he will not survive? All happened by God's will.

How many Saints does your church have? Everyone will say, a lot. How did those people become Saints? Where they all without sin - when: *"All have sinned and come short of the glory of God."(Romans 3:23)* So all Saints were sinners but yet hundreds if not thousands are today in God's Kingdom living an eternal and blessed life. St. Demetrius, St. Barbara, St. George, St. Nicholas, St. Paul, St. John, St. Volodymyr and thousands of others are with God today. Many of them were tortured and martyred for Christ. Others just by their earthly and holy life which they led on earth became Saints by the will of God, even though they were sinners like all of us.

When we see evil around us, we always say that it is the devil's work. Maybe it is, but the question is by whose will, by whose permission? The devil did much harm and evil to Job, but by whose will? We read in the Old Testament: *"Am I now come up without the Lord against this place to destroy it? The Lord said to me, Go up against this land and destroy it." (II Kings 18:25)* and *(Isaiah 36:10)*. Did you see what God said? *"Go up against this land and destroy it."* (II Kings 18:25) God giving orders to destroy by His will. God is All Mighty, All Knowing and only He is the One that can bless and destroy by His will. This world will one day be destroyed as it was during Noah's time. The day when it happens no one knows, but by whose will, will this earth be destroyed? Before that day of destruction comes, we can still change our way of life to inherit His Kingdom.

Do not put off till tomorrow to await the end of times, because the end may come sooner than you think. It may come today, tonight or the next day, maybe in a week, a year or even a thousand years from today. Of that day nor hour knows no one, for even Christ Himself does not know as He says: *"But of that day and that hour knows no man, no, not the Angels which are in heaven, neither the Son, but the Father." (Mark 13:32)* So even God's Son does not know when He will return back to earth in His glory. But today so many people each and every day predict when the end will come. Many have predicted that the end was to be on such and such a day or year. That day and year came and went and the world is still here. The end has come for many of those who had made predictions, but the end of the world has not yet come. No one knows when that will happen. When the Son does not know, nor the Angels in heaven, how can a sinful weakling man on earth know when the end will be? The end will come by God's will, not ours. Until that time comes, do as Jesus said: *"Take heed, watch and pray: for ye know not when the time comes." (Mark 13:33)*

As already mentioned, all things are by the will of God, for even Apostle Paul says: *"And all things are of God." (II Corinthians 5:18)* Paul does not say only good or bad things, he says **all things** are of God. Apostle Paul mentions for the second time that all things come from God by saying: *"For as the woman is of the man, even so is the man also by the woman: but all things of God." (I Corinthians 11:12)* In other places we read the same things. We read: *"The Lord hath made all things, for Himself: yea even the wicked for the day of evil." (Proverbs 16:4)* More of the same is written: *"For of Him, and through Him, and to Him are all things: to whom be glory for ever." (Romans 11:36)* Once again Paul mentions in Corinthians which is God's will when he says: *"But to us there is but one God, the Father, of whom are all things." (I Corinthians 8:6)*

People love good, but at the same time there are many people who love evil. Does the Bible not say that? *"Sinners also love those that love them." (Luke 6:32)* When evil does come, people swear and curse as if it were their world and they owned it. We must remember that God does not do or give only good things. He tries people out, He tries out their faith and trust in Him, in different ways. In the Old Testament we read how God does things so people would fear before Him: *"I know that, whatsoever God does, it shall be forever: nothing can be put to it, nor anything taken away from it: And God does it, that men should fear before Him." (Ecclesiastes 3:14).*

God loves us and He does both good and evil to us to teach us that we may fear Him. Just as mentioned previously, when parents punish their children, is it because they hate their child? No. It is because they love their child and with that love they want to train and bring up the child to be better to have respect and bring honour to their parents and God. God is the same. He is an ever loving God, He loves us and He wants us to love Him, to glorify and respect Him. He will do and give good or bad for our lives because that is His will. We ask in the Lord's Prayer that: *"Thy will be done on earth as it is in heaven."* So if we are asking that God's will be done here on earth as it is also in heaven, then why are we pushing that our will be done and not His? If you ask God for something, then let His will be done.

Another good question would be to ask yourself: Who created you and by whose will? We know that two people of opposite sex unite so a human being may be born. People are born in such union, but only by God's will. By whose will was Christ conceived in the womb of the Holy Virgin Mary, the Mother of God? By whose will was John the Baptist conceived in the womb of Elizabeth who was already old and past the age of child bearing. And by whose will was the first man and woman created on earth? *"And God said, Let us make man in our image, after our likeness."* *(Genesis 1:26)* God only had to think, and what He wished, it was done and nothing was, is and will be impossible for Him. Was it Adam's wish or will that Eve was created? She was created by God's will as was Adam. *"And the Lord God said, It is not good that man should be alone, I will make him a help meet for him."* *(Genesis 2:18)* It was God's will to create man and woman.

We have seen and heard of many childless couples. Why did they have no family? Was it their will? Probably in all circumstances not, than by whose will was there no family to these married couples? It was God's will. By whose will, again I ask, was it that Elizabeth in her old age bore John the Baptist? Then on the other hand we have seen families with 3, 6, 10 and at times even more children in one family. (In one congregation I buried an elderly lady who had twenty-one children in her life.) One married couple wishes children, but they have none, another couple wishes not to have any, but they have an abundance of them. By whose will? God steers the world and people on it by His will.

I remember how in one town in one province there was a married couple. They were married twelve years and had no family. They decided to adopt a child. They were fortunate and they got a child through adoption when it was just an infant. The child grew and they were very happy. One day when the child was twelve years old, the father went with his adopted son to load grain unto a truck. He was going to sell the grain in town. The father backed the truck to the granary, started the auger and himself was on the truck shovelling the grain. When the truck was nearing the full mark, suddenly the grain stopped coming from the auger. The man knew that the granary was full, so he thought maybe something happened in the granary that blocked the grain. He looked over the back of the truck and there was his son. He was already dead. Killed instantly when he must have bent to near over the auger to see the grain. His clothing got caught and he died instantly on the spot. By whose will did this tragedy happen? By the will of the father, the neighbours or who? Only by the will of God.

People in that area later were talking that God had meant it and willed for that family to be childless. They had no children of their own and the one they adopted, twelve years later God took that one away too. So we ask by whose will? Someone will argue and say that it was the devil's work that the young lad was killed. Yet how interesting to know- whose authority does the devil have to take peoples lives? Only God can take a life. How many people tried to commit suicide and failed, because God's will was that they still live. God gave permission to the devil to do as he pleased with Job, but as to the soul, that belongs to God, *"The Lord said unto Satan, Behold, he is in thine hand: but save his life." (Job 2:6)* The devil was happy and joyful, for he thought he would now for sure win Job over to his side, but he could not and did not.

Yes it's the devil that does evil, but can God not stop the devil from doing evil to innocent people any time the devil tries to push his way into hurting people? But yet how many times have we read that God says He will do evil to people, punishing them for their sins. My late mother used to say that God will not come down from heaven with a stick or lash and start beating us. No, He will send other punishments upon us like hail, tornadoes, hurricanes, drought, floods, earthquakes, illnesses, diseases, etc., etc. That is the kind of punishments God will give us.

When Christ came to the two men possessed by the demons, Christ didn't wait a week or a month to chase the demons out. He immediately fulfilled the devil's request and made the two men well again, by whose will? Read about it in *Matthew 8:28-32.* After this incident happened, Christ again did not wait to help two blind men. *"And when Jesus departed thence, two blind men followed Him crying, and saying, Thou Son of David, have mercy on us. And when He was come into the house, the blind men came to Him: and Jesus saith unto them, Believe ye that I am able to do this? They said unto Him, Yea, Lord. Then touched He their eyes, saying, according to your faith be it unto you." (Matthew 9:27-29)* God can do anything He wishes, any time He wishes.

Why do we see some people that are rich and well off and others are poor, while still others are even homeless? They may be living across the street one from the other as we read in the story of Lazarus and a rich man. Both neighbourly families may be working as hard as they can. Maybe they even go to church every Holy Day, yet one family is rich and another is poor. And yet it is God's will that the rich help the poor. It is God's will that He wants people's hearts to be softened and be merciful to the poor. When the flood came in Winnipeg, Manitoba and the Ice Storm in Quebec and Ontario, those people became very unfortunate and helpless, but other people came to their aid. After tornadoes, hurricanes, earthquakes or other misfortunes happen, do people not rush out to help? By whose will do all these things happen or occur?

Any good or harm that comes to people and this world in which we live comes from the will of God. We read: *"I know that whatsoever God does, it shall be for ever: nothing can be put to it, nor anything taken from it: And God does it, that men should fear before Him." (Ecclesiastes 3:14)* Whatever God does, man can't control it. Man cannot stop an earthquake, a tornado, a hurricane or any other catastrophe that may strike the world. God has a will and we have a will, but God's will is stronger then ours. We may attempt to do something, and God's will may let it go ahead or He may prevent it.

I have an idea, but I don't think anyone would listen to me. But let me try. Yes we have tornadoes coming along killing people and causing damage. Can we not try to stop that tornado? How? Well when we see tornado weather is forming and approaching, get a plane up into the air with and explosive rocket or bomb on board. When a tornado is forming, get the plane to that area and shoot that rocket or bomb into the tornado that it explode inside the tornado. Someone may laugh at this suggestion, but has anyone ever tried this to see if it would work? If that works, why not do it and save lives and damage.

We heard from the Holy Bible and probably witnessed many times in our lives how an older parent puts their hope in their only child. They have belief and faith that when they die, their child will bury them. But how many times have we seen, it happen the other way, the child dies and the old and aged mother, a widow is left alone on the face of the earth. The parent is left to bury their child in who they had put their hope and trust. Who will care for them when they are aged and can hardly fare for themselves? By whose will does such an incident happen? We read about this same thing that happened in Christ's time when a young man died and the mother was left alone and Christ resurrected her son. *(Luke 7:11-15)* Every time anything good or evil happens, it can only happen because of God's will. *(Ecclesiastes 3:14)*

In today's society where everything goes, people don't even think of God. They hardly ever talk about Him. They barely ever mention His name unless only in profanity and swearing. They don't think that one day this same God that they don't want to know will repay them with punishment for their way of life they conduct today on this earth. Someone may jump up and protest, that God would not punish people, because He is a merciful God. Yes He is a merciful God. God is merciful, but are parents not merciful to their children and still they punish them when they step out of line? Sometimes a parent is ready to punish their child, but at the last moment will change their mind. God does the same. Was He not willing to spare Sodom and Gomorrah if only so many righteous people could be found?

God spoke to the disobedient people saying: *"Then will I also walk contrary unto you, and will punish you yet seven times for your sins." (Leviticus 26:24)* Again in the same book of Moses we read: *"Then I will walk contrary unto you in fury; and I, even I, will chastize you seven times for your sins." (Leviticus 26:28)* And God will show His anger for our sins as He says: *"And I will destroy your high places, and cut down your images, and cast your carcases upon the carcases of your idols, and my soul shall abhor you." (Leviticus 26:30)* How many times we see God's anger upon His people and His earth that He created because people do not abide by His Commandments. Before God gets really furious upon His people, do you not think people should change their ways of life to escape God's punishment?

In the Holy Scriptures we read: *"And the Lord repented of the evil which He thought to do unto His people."(Exodus32:14)* God had punishment all planned for His people when Moses was up in the mountain and received the Ten Commandments, but He "repented," changed, became merciful. If people repent and change from their sins, God forgives them their iniquities. In the same manner do people forgive others as we say in the Lord's

Prayer. At times God punishes people and when people repent, He will ease their punishment or reward them with His blessings. God sent a pestilence on the people of Israel and Jerusalem and after a number of people died, God called the Angel back. *"So the Lord sent a pestilence upon Israel from the morning even to the time appointed: And there died of the people from Dan even to Beersheba seventy thousand men. And when the Angel stretched out his hand upon Jerusalem to destroy it, the Lord repented him of the evil, and said to the Angel that destroyed the people. It is enough: stay now thine hand."* (II Samuel 24:15-16) and (I Chronicles 21:14-15)

We think that anything that is bad or evil is not of God. How many times have we read in the Bible that God did evil, to harm or destroy people or things? *"Thus saith the Lord, Behold I will bring evil unto this place and upon the inhabitants thereof."* (II Chronicles 34:24) By whose will? In another place we again see God bringing evil upon David: *"Thus saith the Lord, Behold, I will raise up evil against thee out of thine own house and I will take thy wives before thine eyes, and give them unto thy neighbour, and he shall lie with thy wives in the sight of this sun."* (II Samuel 12:11) In another place we find and read of God doing evil when we read *II Kings 22:16-20.* Often we read how God commanded or told someone to go and destroy and do harm and damage to people and property. *"Am I now come up without the Lord against this place to destroy it? The Lord said to me, Go up against this land, and destroy it."* (II Kings 18:25) (Isaiah 36:10) By whose will? Again we read of God's evil and destruction in the Book of Jeremiah when God tells the people what to do, for He will bring harm to the area: *"Set up the standard toward Zion: retire, stay not: for I will bring evil from the north, and a great destruction."* (Jeremiah 4:6)

God's anger can bring great destruction upon mankind. God commanded people to honour the Sabbath and if they don't then they can expect suffering for it. *"Behold if ye will not hearken unto me to hallow the Sabbath day, and not to bear a burden, even entering in at the gates of Jerusalem on the Sabbath day: then I will kindle a fire in the gates thereof, and it shall devour the palaces of Jerusalem, and it shall not be quenched." (Jeremiah 17:27)*

By whose will did all those evil things happen? All done by God's will. God has evil awaiting to befall mankind, if man does not repent and listen to His word and obey it. *"Thus saith the Lord of hosts, the God of Israel: Behold, I will bring upon this city and upon all her towns all the evil that I have pronounced against it, because they have hardened their necks that they might not hear My words." (Jeremiah 19:15)*

All kinds of evil can befall man: floods, earthquakes, famines, tornadoes, pestilence, etc. God can let loose any one of such catastrophes upon His people for not obeying His laws. *"Thus saith the Lord of hosts, Behold, evil shall go forth from nation to nation, and a great whirlwind shall be raised up from the coasts of the earth." (Jeremiah 25:32)* We listen to the radio, watch TV and read newspapers and find that another hurricane is approaching land with heavy winds and pouring down heavy rains. We look at satellite pictures that are taken from 200-300 miles in space and we see great big circling clouds which is the hurricane. We see the eye of the storm approaching land.

People board up their windows in their homes and business and are evacuated by hundreds of thousands of cars on the road. We call the approaching storm a hurricane. God calls them "a great whirlwind," as we read in the Bible. The hurricane or "great whirlwind" comes inland from the "Coasts of the earth," killing people and doing millions of dollars of damage and destroying everything in its path. Then next time when we turn on our radio or TV and we hear that a tornado has ripped through a part of a state or province killing people and millions of dollars of damage left behind. This tornado is nothing more then what God calls it as a "great whirlwind." God sends these "great whirlwinds" upon people and the earth, for the simple reason, that people have made themselves gods or made their wealth, fortune, career, etc., as a god and forgot the real God who created this world and everything on it. Man has forgotten God's Commandments and made his own laws without God. The Lord's Prayer has been taken out of schools. People have forgotten how to pray. People go about their daily lives without even thinking once that God can see their every move they make each day. People made sports spectacles as their gods on Sundays(holy days). There are more people at sports spectacles then there are in churches. Each year more churches are being closed up and more money spent to build and rebuild sports facilities, bars, salons, recreation facilities, etc. And God can see everything that people do and to remind people to think and look to Him, He keeps sending upon the people "great whirlwinds."

Man today can't find time for God anymore. He became god himself and wants others to respect him, obey him and do as he wants, and not as God wants. Man is to occupied with sports, good times, making money, pleasure, sex, partying and has no time for God and church. All these things go on day after day but not for a moment does one stop to think how they came to have what they have - health, family, home, wealth, etc.

God tells us not to seek for those things: *"And seeks thou great things for thyself? Seek them not: for behold I will bring evil upon all flesh, saith the Lord: but thy life will I give unto thee for a prey in all places whither thou goes." (Jeremiah 45:5)* People worry and hurry to stock up on food, clothing and on all sorts of pleasure, money into the savings banks and buy every kind of gadget they may see and want. In the New Testament we hear Christ telling and warning us: *"Therefore take no thought, saying, what shall we eat? Or What shall we drink? Or, Wherewithal shall we be clothed? But seek ye first the Kingdom of God, and His righteousness; and all these things shall be added unto you." (Matthew 6:33)*

Jesus also tells us: *"Behold the fowls of the air: for they sow not, neither do they reap, nor gather into barns: yet your heavenly Father feeds them. Are ye not much better than they?"(Matthew 6:26)* Christ plainly warns us and gives advice what we are to do. He says that birds do not seed, they don't harvest, they don't store and yet God looks after them. Are they worth more then we are? Why then does man whom God created to love, honour and respect Him, turned away from Him? We cannot serve two mammon. You can't say that I look after sports all day and all week long and have only half an hour a week for God. You can't say that you have to work five days a week and don't have time for God. You work five days a week and God said that we should work six days a week and the seventh day to give for God. God said that no one shall work on the Sabbath, not even an animal, because that day belongs to God.

By God's will we receive from Him all good and evil, every thing we deserve for our actions, and cannot complain and say that the world is not treating us fairly. The evil things which happened before, they are happening today and they will happen tomorrow, or until such time that man turns back to live God's way. Joshua was told by God what would happen if the people do not listen and obey the Lord: *"Therefore it shall come to pass that as all good things come upon you which the Lord your God promised you: so shall the Lord bring upon you all evil things, until He has destroyed you from off this good land which the Lord your God hath given you." (Joshua 23:15)* God will give us good things, but He will also destroy them if we neglect Him and live without Him.

God gave good things to Joshua and His people and He also gives good things for us each day, but He can also take everything away by His will, permitting the devil to destroy things which God can also do Himself. We remember when in Edmonton some people had beautiful homes and then suddenly the homes started falling over the banks into the river. We remember how the hurricane Andrew and others came out of the ocean into the land and destroyed everything. We remember how over 15,000 people died in an earthquake in Turkey. We remember of the lives lost and millions dollars of damage done from monsoons in the pacific. God gave people everything, but He can also take everything away. Did not the same thing happen to righteous Job? God had given Job everything, but then by God's will the devil took everything away from Job. God told Joshua that He promised him all good things and gave them to him, but God also said; *"So shall the Lord bring upon you all evil things." (Joshua 23:15)*

God not only through His will gives and takes things from us, but He can also destroy everything as He did with all the people on earth with a deluge, as He did to Sodom and Gomorrah, as He did with the Tower of Babylon, as He destroyed the Egyptians in the Red Sea when they came after Moses and His people. God by His will can use vengeance against us for not obeying Him. *"What is God, willing to show His wrath, and to make His power known endured with much long suffering the vessels of wrath fetted to destruction?" (Romans 9:22)* God with His will can destroy as well as build, as we learn from the Holy Scriptures. Christ will come again to judge us at which time the world shall be destroyed. We know from the Holy Scriptures that Jesus will not come back Himself by His will, but by the will of His Father: *"I can of My own self do nothing; as I hear I judge: and My judgement is just; because I seek not Mine own will, but the will of the Father which hath sent Me." (John 5:30)* Even when Christ was on earth He did things by His Father's will. He resurrected the dead, gave sight to the blind, made the lame walk, made wine from water, fed more than five thousand people with fives loaves of bread and two fishes, etc.

In the Book of Leviticus we read of God sending warnings to the disobedient. He warns us what we may expect if we don't listen and obey Him. He will see that we are slain before our enemy.

(Leviticus 26:17) He will punish us seven times more for our sins. *(Leviticus 26:18)* Our pride of power will be broken. *(Leviticus 26:19)* Our strength will vanish and the earth will not produce its fruit. *(Leviticus 26:20)* Still if people will not repent and turn to God, He will bring seven times more plagues. *(Leviticus 26:21)*. Wild beasts will kill our children, cattle and us. *(Leviticus 26:22)* God will send pestilence upon us. *(Leviticus 26:25)*

For our sins, God will be ready to punish us up to seven times. *(Leviticus 26:28)* God's fury and wrath will be upon the earth by His will because people do not want to obey Him. All this we can read in Leviticus chapter 26. Someone may say that those things happened in the Old Testament and when Christ came things changed. But God did not change. God is still the same, and has not changed. *"Jesus Christ the same yesterday, and today, and for ever." (Hebrews 13:8)* So do you think that another god has come and taken the place of the One that created you?

There are other people that will stand up and argue that what was in the Old Testament is not for us today, because we live in a different and modern world. Some will say that the rules have changed and Christ died for our sins, so we are free. But what did Christ say when He was on earth and talked to His Apostles? *"Think not that I came to destroy the law or the prophets: I am come not to destroy, but to fulfil."(Matthew 5:17)* The laws that God gave in the Old Testament are forever. He has not changed them. Has God changed the Ten Commandments? If He did, He hasn't told anyone to this date that it has changed. Has He told you that He has changed His Commandments? Only those that want to be gods themselves change laws to suit themselves, so they would not have to answer to God for breaking His laws. But when Christ comes again, we will all stand before Him to answer for our life on earth. In the other world you will not be asking God questions, God will do the asking and you will have to do the answering. Answers that God accepts are like if you were the poor Lazarus who was homeless from the Bible as we read. Your answers if you were sick or bed ridden and could not come to church or help, that will be a good answer for God. But if you try to wiggle and find some other useless answer, God will not accept such answers. In our world today a prisoner does not ask the judge questions. The judge and lawyers ask questions.

Today even if all the armies of the world gathered together to battle God, they would still loose the war. God would destroy every warrior. God would not need weapons. He will only think what He wants to happen and it will be fulfilled. God has destroyed others who thought that they could conquer God, but it was to no avail. Hitler thought that he would become god. God destroyed him. Stalin thought that he would become god, but God destroyed him also. Napoleon thought he would be god, but he was also destroyed by God. God will destroy and punish the world for its wickedness. *"And I will punish the world for their evil. And the wicked for their iniquity; and I will cause the arrogance of the proud to cease, and will lay low the haughtiness of the terrible."* *(Isaiah 13:11)* And by whose will, will God do this?

No one can fight and beat God. He is the All Supreme, the one that blesses and punishes. He can do everything. *"I form the light, and create darkness; I make peace, and create evil: I the Lord do all these things." (Isaiah 45:7)* God says that He, "does all these things." He causes peace and He causes war. He causes love and He causes hatred, jealousy, greed, etc. He causes happiness and joy, and He also causes grief and misery. He can do everything for He says so: *"I the Lord do all these things." (Isaiah 45:7)* When my late mother was still living and at times when some catastrophe struck the world, she used to say: "You see, God only raised his little finger and see what happened. What would happen if God raised His whole hand?"

Some people may say they have nothing to lose by the way they live because Jesus died for their sins. But they do have something to lose. They can lose eternal life with God in heaven. Christ died on the cross for our sins, but that didn't give us the right to live and do as we please. We still have to live by God's Commandments. Some people say that all they have to do is believe in Jesus Christ and they will be saved. Is it really that easy and simple? Is that all there is to life? I can do as I please, believe in Jesus and go to heaven?

Do you mean to tell me that tonight I can go and murder someone and tomorrow tell you that I believe in Jesus and will go to heaven? Do you think that if next week I broke into your home, beat you up and your family, take your belongings, then next day say that I believe in Jesus, I will be saved? Do you really think that if I went and burned down your home tonight, that tomorrow I can say I believe in Jesus and go to heaven? Do you really think that if I went around each day and night and sexually assaulted people, then say I believe in Jesus and I will go to heaven? Do you really think that if I went around and told the untruth and made up false stories about you, then turned around and said that I believe in Jesus I will be saved? Think about it again, those of you who say that you only have to believe in Jesus to be saved. It is not that easy to get to heaven, just by believing in Jesus, have faith and be saved.

Apostle James who was taught by Christ Himself, gives us a different version of believing. He says: *"What doth it profit, my brother though a man say he hath faith, and have not works? Can faith save him? (James 2:14)* He goes on farther and tells us: *"Even so faith, if it hath not works is dead being alone." (James 2:17)* A man can't just go on living on this earth and not doing anything worthwhile for his fellow man or neighbour, yet say that he believes, and has faith in Jesus Christ and will go to heaven for eternity. Apostle James warns us by saying: *"But wilt thy know, O vain man, that faith without works is dead." (James 2:20)* To live as you live by your will and doing whatever you care to do, have faith and no-good works to support your faith, then your faith is useless and in vain, for Apostle James tells us: *"For as the body without the spirit is dead, so faith without works is dead also." (James 2:26)*

Living on earth, breaking God's laws and commandments, and saying that I have faith and believe in Jesus Christ and that I will be saved, is like talking to the wind. Such talk is worthless and useless. Apostle James tells us: *"For whosoever shall keep the whole law, and yet offend in one point, he is guilty of all." (James 2:10)* You break one law, and you have broken them all. Yes we are all sinners, but just to go on sinning and having no good works, cannot save anyone as Apostle James says. You may think that you haven't killed anyone, stolen anything, assaulted anyone, that you are free from sin. But Apostle Paul says differently. *"For all have sinned, and come short of the glory of God." (Romans 3:23)*

God rewards us with good, but also punishes us with evil and misfortune for breaking His laws. In the Old Testament we read: *"But the Spirit of the Lord departed from Saul, and an evil spirit from the Lord troubled him. (I Samuel 16:14).* How much more plainer can it get when we read: *"And an evil spirit from the Lord troubled him."* We thought that God only did good things. Well what then is an *"evil spirit from the Lord?"* And you thought that God is only a Good Spirit?

"An evil spirit from the Lord," says the Holy Scripture. By God's will the evil spirit went into Saul. How about Apostle Paul writing in the New Testament, what does he have to say? Did he not have, *"A thorn in the flesh?" (II Corinthians 12:7)* We do not know what kind of a thorn was bothering him. Was it some physical ailment that he had? But he goes on to say that he asked God to take that thorn away from him. *"For this thing I besought the Lord thrice that it might depart from me. And He said unto me, My grace is sufficient for thee: for My strength is made perfect in weakness."(II Corinthians 12:8-9)* Satan had given Paul the pain of

whatever it was that bothered him. Satan gave Paul the thorn by God's will, for God said that; *"My grace is sufficient for thee."*

God punishes and will punish people by whose will? God says: *"But I will punish you according to the fruit of your doings; saith the Lord." (Jeremiah 21:14)* By whose will? If God is a kind and merciful God, how come He speaks out in so many places in the Holy Scriptures that He will punish people for their doings? But He is merciful to those who repent and live by His laws. God knows that we are all sinners, but if a person does not want to live by God's way, then God has no other choice, but to send His punishment upon us. But then by whose will does God punish us or will punish us? Is it by the will of the Angels in heaven? Is it by the will of the Virgin Mary? Is it by the will of the Saints in heaven? By whose will does God punish people? Only by His will He sends down upon us the punishments that we deserve from Him. But He can always change the punishments into blessings if man will first repent and change his ways of living to respect, obey, honour and thank God.

When Moses brought God's chosen people out of Egypt, the people wandered around in the wilderness for forty years. That area today, you can drive around with the car in a few hours or a day. The place was desert like and they did not till the land, irrigate the soil or produce food for forty years, yet they were fed each day. How? *"And the children of Israel did eat manna forty years, until they came to a land inhabited; they did eat manna until they came unto the borders of the land of Canaan." (Exodus 16:35)*

Again the question comes to mind, by whose will did Israel survive for forty years in the wilderness without having to work for food? Every morning when they awakened, manna was already waiting for them and all they did was pick it up and consume it. *"And when the dew that lay was gone up, behold, upon the face of the wilderness there lay a small round thing, as small as the hoar frost on the ground. And when the children of Israel saw it, they said one to*

another, It is manna; for they wist not what it was. And Moses said
unto them; This is the bread which the Lord hath given you to eat."
(Exodus 14:15)

While mentioning Moses, again let us ask the question; by
whose will did Moses receive the Ten Commandments? Was
it by his will? Was it his brother Aaron's will? Was it by the
will of the Israelites? It was by God's will that He gave the Ten
Commandments and like everything else it was, is and will be done
and created by God's will. God gave the Ten Commandments not
only for the children of Israel, but all people on earth. When the
year 2000 began to draw nearer each day, we heard more and
more that it will be the end of the world in the year 2000. We
are assured that the end will come, but does anyone really know
when the end will be? Absolutely not.

We know that Jesus lived on earth, was crucified, ascended
into heaven from whence He will again one day return to this
earth in His glory. In The Creed we read: "And He will come
again to judge the living and the dead." To know that He will
return to earth again, we go back to the Apostolic times, to the
day when Christ was ascending into heaven and the Apostles
stood with amazement and watched what was happening. *"And
when He had spoken these things, while they beheld, He was taken
up: and a cloud received Him out of their sight, And while they looked
steadfastly toward heaven as He went up, behold two men stood by
them in white apparel: which also said; ye men of Galilee, why stand
ye gazing up into heaven? This same Jesus, which is taken up from
you into heaven, shall so come in like manner as ye have seen Him go
into heaven." (Acts 1:9-11)*

We are told that this same Jesus will return back to earth
in the same glory He went up, but it does not say when He will
return. We don't know when He will return for He Himself
said: *"But of that day and hour knows no man, no, not the Angels
of heaven, but My Father alone." (Matthew 24:36)* According to

these words, even Jesus does not know when He is to return for He says that only His Father knows. How then can sinful man in today's world know and be so sure that this Jesus will return in 2000? How about all the other people who had predicted that the end of the world was to come at such and such a time, but it didn't. Now that time had come and gone but the world is still here. What probably has come to an end is the life on earth for those who predicted the end of the world. No man knows when the end will come. We only know that it is coming, because when it comes it will be unexpected. What did Christ say about the coming? *"Then shall two be in the field; the one shall be taken, and the other left. Two women shall be grinding at the mill; the one shall be taken, and the other left. Watch therefore: for ye not know what hour your Lord comes." (Matthew 24:40-42)*

We know that the end is nearing and comes closer each day, only we don't know when. Christ gave us some notice or what the signs will be before He comes back. He said: *"And many false prophets shall rise, and shall deceive many." (Matthew 24:11)* The Jonestown massacre, the Waco, Texas turbulence and others around the world led many people to their demise. He said that: *"For many shall come in My name, saying, I am Christ; and shall deceive many." (Matthew 24:5)*

How many people are being deceived today? We have thousands of sects each one claiming that they are the Christ and they are the true believers. There are many deposed and forgotten sects now, but where are their leaders today? What about the Evangelist preachers in the USA? How many have brought scandal upon themselves and their followers? How many of them at times stood up at a pulpit and screamed at the top of their lungs that they are right and know everything. Where are they today? How many have been dethroned from their high horse that they sat upon? Still even today, how many others are leading people away from Christ, away from God? One sign we know that

Christ will be returning back to earth is what He himself told us. *"And ye shall hear of wars and rumours of wars: see that ye are not troubled: for all these things must come to pass, but the end is not yet." (Matthew 24:6)* How many wars have been fought and how many are in progress today as we speak, since Christ spoke those words? Today we still have wars on the face of this earth and yet Christ said: "The end is not yet."

More warnings from Christ were: *"For nation shall rise against nation, and kingdom against kingdom: and there shall be famines, and pestilence, and earthquakes, in divers places. All these are the beginning of sorrows." (Matthew 24:7-8)* How many nations have attacked other nations and even today as we speak this is happening. Chechnya, Africa, Kosovo, Middle East, Indonesia, Iraq and others. Nation attacking another nation, and many nations attacking one nation (Serbia, Afghanistan, Iraq).

Of how many famines have we heard in the past two-three decades? How about the Great Depression even in North America in the 1930's? How many people went hungry to bed each night? Then what about the earthquakes? Each time you turn on your radio or TV and another earthquake has occurred in some part of this world. Today people know that the western part of North America will be shaken very seriously by an earthquake and everyone is talking about the coming of "The big one."All these happenings of earthquakes, Christ told us two thousand years ago that they would happen, but He said that all this is, "The beginning of sorrows." All these things tell us that the end is getting closer each day, only we don't know when it will be. All this is happening by whose will? Yes by the will of God, and yet people do not want to listen and obey Him.

Christ's other words of warning are: *"Then will they deliver you up to be afflicted, and shall kill you: And ye shall be hated of all nations for My name's sake." (Matthew 24:9)* What happened in Ukraine in 1932-33? More than 7,000,000 perished in the man-made famine. What happened during the Second World War? How many people lost their lives, homes, families? What happened to Christ's churches and the clergy in Ukraine during the Second World War? Tens of bishops were executed. Hundreds of priests were tortured and murdered. Thousands of people perished from the hands of the communist regime. How many churches were destroyed? Crosses were pulled down from the top of the church domes. Churches were burned, bombed, ransacked and many were converted into storage sheds, barns, etc. What happened to the Serbians during the Second World War when 2,000,000 people were tortured and died. All this that happened was foretold by Christ 2000 years ago, with people dying *"For My sake." (Matthew 24:9)*

Another prediction of Christ was: *"And then shall many be offended, and shall betray one another, and shall hate one another." (Matthew 24:10)* Today you can't say a word without offending someone. How far does one have to go today, to find the fulfilment of this prophesy? Neighbour can't get along with neighbour over two inches of property fence lines. Brother can't get along with his brother. Hatred from each and every way you turn. One country hates another. One family lives in hatred with another, and all because of greed and jealousy. Families quarrel and fight because of monetary wealth left by dying family members. To know more about the signs of Christ's coming and the end of this world, read chapter 24 in Matthew, Mark chapter 13:1-13 and Luke 21:5-36. No one knows when Christ will come, but we are assured that He will come. By whose will shall Christ return back to earth again? By God's will, not yours or mine nor anyone else.

So when Christ comes: "He will judge the living and the dead" as we say in the Creed. and as the Holy Scriptures tell us: *"I can of Mine own self do nothing; as I hear, I judge: and My judgement is just." (John 5:30)* How will He judge? For what? Will He judge us for how many automobiles we have? Will it be what kind of a house we have? Will He judge us by the amount of money we have in the bank? Will He judge us by how many university degrees we have? Will He judge us by how many hours a week we worked? Will we be judged by the amount of fish we caught, how many golf games we played, or how many times we went hunting? No, none of this. To find out what we will be judged for, we need to turn to chapter 25 of Matthew and read verses 31-46.

The Holy Bible says: *"When the Son of man shall come in His glory, and all the holy Angels with Him, then shall He sit upon the throne of His glory: And before Him shall be gathered all nations: And He shall separate them one from another, as a shepherd divides his sheep from the goats." (Matthew 25:31-32)* By whose will shall the nations be gathered and then separated? The Bible says: "When the Son of man comes." The Bible does not say when, no date, no time, nothing. Just meaning that people have to be ready for the coming of Christ at any time. Then another very important thing we read in the passage is: "All nations." Jesus said that everybody that walks on the face of this earth will stand before Him for judgement.

Jesus does not say that only the Irish, or the Ukrainians, or the Japanese, or the English will gather before Him. He says that, "All nations" will come. It does not matter whether you believe in Christ or not, you will be there before Him on judgement day. It does not matter whether you are Christian, Moslem, Jew or any other faith or belief, you will still be there before Christ on judgement day for "all nations shall be gathered" and not only one or two. Everyone that lives and walks the face of this earth belongs to some nation. He belongs to some country, either by birth or citizenship. You, I and everyone will be standing there before Christ on judgement day, and by whose will? Will it be your will, mine or someone else? No, it will be by God's will that we will stand before Him and be judged.

The first thing that will happen is that Christ will appear on earth as a king with all His Angels. The Angels will be Christ's heavenly army. He will separate the sinners from the righteous people. The sinners will be on His left and the righteous on His right. To those on His right He will say: *"Come, ye blessed of My Father, inherit the kingdom prepared for you from the foundation of the world." (Matthew 25:34)* By His will, He has prepared a kingdom for those on Christ's right side. These were the people that helped others and are now getting their reward for it. Jesus says: *"For I was hungered, and ye gave Me meat: For I was thirsty and ye gave Me drink: I was a stranger, and ye took Me in: Naked, and you clothed Me: I was sick, and ye visited Me: I was in prison and ye came unto Me." (Matthew 25:35-36)*

That is what we will be judged for. Did we feed the hungry? Visited the sick? Did we supply clothing for the needy and so forth? If we did, Christ's reward and payment will be life with Him in His Father's Kingdom, for He says: *"Verily I say unto you, Inasmuch as ye have done it unto one of the least of these My brethren, ye have done it unto Me." (Matthew 25:40)* So whatever you did in your lifetime for any person on this earth, Christ says that you did it for Him.

But what about those on Christ's left, what kind of reward do they get? What payment do they get for their life on earth? Christ says: *"Then He shall say also unto them on His left hand. Depart from Me, ye cursed, into everlasting fire, prepared for the devil and his angels: For I was hungered, and ye gave Me no meat; I was thirsty, and ye gave Me no drink; I was a stranger and ye took Me not in: naked and ye clothed Me not: sick and in prison, and ye visited Me not." (Matthew 25:41-43)*

These kind of people Jesus calls, "cursed" and sends them off into "everlasting fire." These people will stand up in protest to Christ and say: *"Lord, when saw we Thee hungry, or athirst, or a stranger, or naked, or sick, or in prison, and did not minister unto Thee?"(Matthew 25:44)* They are demanding, as we say in other words, why didn't you tell us that you were hungry, naked, thirsty, and then we would have helped You. But Christ replies to them saying: *"Verily I say unto you, Inasmuch as ye did it not to one of the least of these, ye did it not to Me." (Matthew 25:45)*

That means that anytime you did good or evil to anyone of earth, you did that to Christ. We see that the people on Christ's left did not kill anyone, they did not steal anything from anyone, they just lived from day to day minding their own business. But Christ called them, "cursed." Why? Because they only thought of themselves, it will be their greed that will make them cursed. They did not care what else was happening to someone else. They wanted to get as many riches as they could, to save as much as they could, and as we say, "for a rainy day." But the trouble for those people will be that there will be no rainy day in the other world. Because they did not assist, aid or help anyone on earth, and their reward is, "everlasting fire." By whose will?

There will be no lawyers to defend those people in heaven. Wealth, education, food, clothing will have no meaning in the other world. To live with Christ in heaven, today stretch out your hand with help to the poor, hungry, naked, ill. We see that we will all be judged, not by how many bank accounts we have, how many years of university we have, how many hours a week we worked, how much we got paid for doing something, but our judgement will be based on how much we helped the needy. We know that we don't have to help those that are better off then we are, but how many are there that are worst off then us. They are the ones that need help. So by whose will, will we be judged? By God's will, like everything else that happens, happens by His will.

Christ picked out twelve apostles. By whose will where they picked? Was it by their will? Was it by our will? Go to a Christian book store and ask for a book about Christ's Apostles so you may read the book and learn who the Apostles were. Whom did Christ pick out for His Apostles? Where they all professors, engineers, doctors, lawyers, rabbis? No. Christ picked out the poorest people, those with much patience and hard working - fishermen. Just poor, regular fishermen. Apostle Luke was the only one that had some education being a doctor by trade or profession. All other Apostles were just ordinary day to day workers, fishermen who were striving from one day to the next just to support their families. Yet, these that Christ picked out, changed the world. With God's help and His will, Christ's church spread to every corner of the earth. Just regular fishermen became Christ's right-hand men and helpers.

There must have been a reason why Christ didn't pick out trained and educated, professional men to be His Apostles. It was God's will that they were chosen, by Christ Himself. No one helped Christ to pick out His Apostles. Why didn't He pick out rich and well to do people? He knew that it would be hard to convince the rich to give up their wealth and make them His Apostles, for later He told them: *"Verily I say unto you, That a rich man shall hardly enter into the Kingdom of heaven." (Matthew 19:23)* That was not all that He told His Apostles about the wealthy people. He told them: *"And again I say unto you, it is easier for a camel to go through the eye of a needle, than for a rich man to enter into the kingdom of God." (Matthew 19:24)*

Another important topic that could be debated is, what has been forgotten in most countries - the death penalty. This used to be a hot topic at one time. The government got mixed into religion, made their own laws, while at the same time throwing out God's laws. When we talk about the death penalty for people who commit murder, today that death penalty has been abolished in Canada and some other countries. Some people say that is the way it should have been done a long time ago. The death penalty has become a sentence in prison for a number of years, so that the murderer can be fed and looked after, while the victims must suffer the rest of their lives. After a number of years the murderer asks for parole and at times gets it so that he can get out of prison and commit more crime, so more people would suffer.

But what does God say and how does He look at someone who is a murderer? Does God have a say in this? Was it not Him who gave the law, *"Thou shalt not kill." (Exodus 20:13)* Does God and should God have a say in this matter, or has man taken away God's right? To know what God has to say about those who kill others, we have to look for answers in God's Holy Book - The Bible.

We will spend a few minutes of time on this topic because in some localities, provinces, states or countries there is still talk going on about the death penalty. This is a serious topic, for murder is a serious thing in the eyes of God who was the first to give us this law. God also gives answers to it. In the Old Testament God gave laws as to what must be done to the murderer. Some will turn immediately and say that what was in the Old Testament does not concern us, because we live in the new world, "A New Age". But was it not Christ was came and began the New Testament saying: *"Think not that I come to destroy the law, or the prophets: I am come not to destroy, but to fulfil." (Matthew 5:17)*

Christ did not destroy the law that His Father gave for us all. It is man who took it upon himself to throw out God's laws and implement his own, opposite to God's law. Why did man change God's laws? He did not like and still does not like to follow what God said so man has made himself a god. The law about punishment or consequences for the murderer still stands today, God has not changed it, not yet. The Bible gives us answers as to the punishment for murderers

In the first book of the Holy Bible we see after the Great Deluge when Noah was saved with his family, that God speaks what the penalty is for the murderer. We read: *"Whosoever sheds man's blood, by man shall his blood be shed: for in the image of God made He man." (Genesis 9:6)* That is very clear, that if someone kills someone, he must also die, so why has man changed God's law? Let us look for more answers to the same topic.

In the Book of Exodus we read: *"He that smites a man, so that he die, shall be surely put to death." (Exodus 21:12)* Here again there is no question as to what the punishment is for a murderer, for God plainly says that, *"he shall be surely put to death."* No two ways about it, plain as the sun from the moon. God is the giver of life and only He can take a life away, but when someone takes a life, God is straight forward and says that the murderer's punishment is also death. The murderer must die like he made someone else die. If it is an accident, that is a different thing, from when someone kills purposely with intention.

God continues to say: *"But if a man come presumptuously upon his neighbour, to slay him with guile: thou shalt take him from Mine altar, that he may die." (Exodus 21:14)* Murderers, God does not even want to know them, He says that they shall be taken away from His altar. He wants nothing to do with them, because they will never inherit His Kingdom. God says plainly that even He cannot save the murderer, so how can man make a law that is greater then God's? It seems that man has lost fear of God and made god himself. In today's world people say: "Everything goes," but for that everything, a person sometimes must pay for his actions.

How many times have you seen, heard or read how children attack their parents. Sometimes parents are beat up by their own adult children and sometimes they are even killed by them. What kind of punishment should be meted out to those kind children? What kind of punishment has God allowed for someone who smites their parents? God says: *"And he that smites his father or his mother, shall be surely put to death." (Exodus 21:15)* WHAT? This is God's plain law and will of what must be done with such children.

God shows us that parenthood is sacred, that if someone kills their parent, it is death to the striker-murderer. It is a serious crime in the eyes of God and He purposely gave that law, that children obey their parents. But, what happens today if the children beat up or kill their parents? They get probation, they get a suspended sentence, maybe they are told not to go near their parents' home, maybe even do some community work, which means nothing to the murderer. SOMETIMES the murderer may even get a small jail sentence. God gave us rules of what the punishment is to be, why has man changed God's law? God strongly says that the murderer: *"shall be surely put to death."* No two ways about it, for God says "surely" and not <u>maybe</u>. God goes another step farther and says: *"And he that curses his father or his mother, shall surely be put to death." (Exodus 21:17)*. Even in the New Testament these same very words Jesus spoke and did not say to change or throw out that law when He said: *"And He said unto them, Full well ye reject the commandment of God, that ye may keep your own tradition. For Moses said, Honour thy father and thy mother; and, Whoso curses father or mother, let him die the death." (Mark 7:9-10)* Christ Himself repeated the law that was given by God and He did not say to change it, so who went against God's law and God's will? Jesus said that if you even curse your parents, the penalty is death.

In the New Testament we read how one day Jesus was approached by the Pharisees and the scribes who were tempting and attacking Him with questions. Jesus answered them saying that they throw out and reject God's words, so they may keep their own traditions. He also said: *"But ye say, If a man shall say to his father or mother, It is Corban, that is to say a gift, by whatsoever than might be profited by me, he shall be free." (Mark 7: 11)*.

That was the law which said that if someone gave a Corban, which meant a gift to God, he was freed from punishment. He could give a gift or sacrifice something after the crime, or he could will it that after he dies, his estate or part of it was given to God. The thing is that God says, just for cursing one's parents, the penalty is: "surely must die." But in the twentieth century, who has given a gift for cursing their parents? Who has given God a gift for killing their parents? No one, for man has made his tradition greater then God's law. We see that God had instituted a very high regard for parents, that if only one were to curse his parents, that was death. *"And he that curses his father, or his mother, shall surely be put to death." (Exodus 21:17)*

Let us look at another law in another book in the Bible. We can read the whole chapter twenty-one in the Book of Exodus for the rules and laws that God gave Moses, for the whole world and up to the present times. God has not yet come down and given new laws in place of those that we have in the Bible.

In another book we read: *"And he that blasphemes the name of the Lord, he shall surely be put to death, and all the congregation shall certainly stone him: as well the stranger, as he that is born in the land, when he blasphemes the name of the Lord shall be put to death." (Leviticus 24:16)* Someone may say that this is a very severe punishment. It is, and it ought to be, because God does not permit anyone to speak evil of Him, to make fun of Him, to curse Him, swear at Him, etc. That was and is God's will that He instituted that law.

Today you see people on the street, at work or anywhere else and what do you hear? You hear swearing, cursing and blaspheming the Lord. God says that the penalty for that is death. How many people have been put to death for blaspheming God? Someone may jump up to defend themselves and say that it's an old law and doesn't stand up today. Those who think and say such things, one day will find out that it is a very important law, but it will be too late for them.

We go on and read: *"And he that kills any man shall surely be put to death." (Leviticus 24:17)* It is the same law that we read in the Book of Exodus. The law is repeated, so it must be an important law. The law has not changed. The penalty is still the same - death. Who got permission from who, to change God's law? God's will was and still is the same today as it was then. God did not change the law, only man wanted to make his own traditions and not to follow God's law. *"And He said unto them, Full well ye reject the commandment of God, that ye may keep your own tradition."(Mark 7:9)*

Farther on we read another verse: *"And he that kills a beast, he shall restore it: and he that kills a man, he shall be put to death."* *(Leviticus 24:21)* No change, verse after verse, verse after verse we read about the same punishment for murderers. God said that the murderer shall be put to death, why is His law not being upheld? Man has changed God's law giving the murderer a "life sentence." Even today in the twenty-first century man has made a mockery of himself. He says that a murderer is given a "life sentence," but 15-20-25 years later you see that same murderer walking the streets and probably thinking how he could commit another murder and get away with it the second time. What kind of a LIFE SENTENCE is it when the murderer is out on the street a few years later? Life means life. What God means is that when someone takes a life, he must die, but man says you go to prison for life, but you can be out on the street a few years later. Is that a life sentence? What kind of laws are these? People change their laws to suit themselves and their traditions. God made His laws and does not change them. If someone is sentenced to life, let it be life, not a few years later and he is as free as the next man. That is wrong, wrong, WRONG. God gave us a law for murderers.

The murderer is fed every day in prison. He has clothes to wear. He pays no taxes. He has all the free time he can think of, yet times come when he begins to riot and upsets the system with his actions in prison. Then the government gives in and lets the prisoner have his way. Why? The prisoner complains, that it is rough and tough being in a prison. If it is so bad in prison, then don't commit any crime and you will not be there. Why do we see so many re-offenders committing crimes when they get out of prison? If it was bad in prison, they would not re-commit the crimes, so as not to be in prison again.

The government spends tons of money to keep murderers in jail. If the government followed God's laws for murderers, the jails and prisons today would be empty. The money spent on the upkeep of the murderers, that money could be spent for health care, education, the homeless, the aged, blind, disabled, victims from the crime, etc. The country could have more doctors, nurses, better hospitals, new schools, more teachers, senior's homes and all kinds of other services for the money spent on murderers if God's law was followed as to the punishment for murderers as God says to do. God gave the commandment: *"Thou shalt not kill." (Exodus 20:13)* If someone does step out past that law, then God has another law as we read in chapters 20 to 23 in Exodus. The Ten Commandments came first and then when people did not obey God's law, He instituted other laws which He has not changed even to the present time.

We have seen from the two books of the Old Testament, Exodus and Leviticus where God says that the punishment for a killer is death. Let us look at another book, Numbers and see what comes even later yet after the Ten Commandments were given. Here we read: *"If he smite him with an instrument of iron, so that he die, he is a murderer: the murderer shall surely be put to death. And if he smite him with a throwing stone, wherewith he may die, and he die, he is a murderer: the murderer shall surely be put to death. Or if he smite him with a hand weapon of wood, wherewith he may die, and he die, he is a murderer: the murderer shall surely be put to death." (Numbers 35:16-18)* Can this law be more clearer what it says as we read it? It is God speaking and His will tells that the punishment for a murderer is the same what he did for someone else - death. There are no if's and but's in God's law. There is no maybe. There is no prison term of a life sentence. God clearly instructs that the, "murderer shall surely be put to death." If that law was up help today, we would need no jails or prisons.

Why then do we keep murderers in prison, feed them, cloth them, look after them and they receive no punishment for their crime as God says it should be? We pay for their food, shelter, clothing, the guards, upkeep of buildings, etc. Millions of dollars are spent on prisoners, while law-abiding people who worked and are working hard, become old, aged, get ill and have no place to end their life because we are short of rooms, beds, doctors, nurses, hospitals, nursing homes, senior homes, etc. They have to suffer out the remaining days of their lives with the bare necessity of care many times in their own homes barely surviving. Today a prison is not a prison anymore. It is not a prison if you are locked up for 15 years, being fed, clothed, no work, all your life free time, smoking permitted, etc. And that is supposed to be a prison?

In Webster's New Twentieth Century Dictionary we find the word prison having a few meanings. One of the meanings on page 1432 says: "A building, usually with cells, where convicted criminals are confined or accused persons are held and awaiting trail: a jail" If it's a place to keep people who are awaiting trial, fine, but once the trial is over, the prisoner is found guilty of murder, why send him back to the same place? It's not what God says to do by His will.

Then another question comes up, who is to put the prisoner to death? God also gave us the answer to that question saying: *"The avenger of blood himself shall slay the murderer: when he meets him, he shall slay him." (Numbers 35:19)* We see so many victims left after the murderer is sent to prison and they have no say in what is to be done with the murderer. They have been victimized for losing a member of their family while the murderer is locked up as we could say to "have a good time." In the meantime the victims go on striving from day to day to earn a piece of bread and they can't seem to find ends to meet in their daily life.

The victims may have lost a husband and father of 2-3 children. Who is going to look after that family, while the prisoner is resting in prison for 20 years or so? Who is going to put food on the table for the small children? Who is going to see that they have clothing on their back and a place to live? Who is going to see that the children have an education? Who will see to it that they may not have to be chased out into the back lane if they cannot support themselves? The prisoner has no worries where his next meal is coming from, or where he is going to sleep tonight. He writes books, watches TV, reads all he wants, has activities, is fed, etc., but who looks after the young widow and children? Who will care for them?

Not to long ago a young police officer was killed in his line of duty in Toronto by two women. He left behind a young wife and children. The two murderers will probably spent 15 years or so in prison not worrying that they will not have any food, or a place to sleep and they will be free again. What about the policeman, why can't he be free? God says very plainly what must happen to murderers. No compassion, nor sorry. Some people may say that the murderers were on drugs and did not know what they were doing. Well that is just too bad with a poor and flimsy excuse. There is no law in Canada that says they had or were forced to take drugs. Who forced them to take drugs? Did someone stand with a gun to their head and force them to use drugs? Just because someone wanted a good time, to be high, they took drugs and killed an innocent person. Now they must pay for the crime God's way, but will they? No.

Again and again God repeats that a murderer must die for his crime. *"Whoso kills any person, the murderer shall be put to death by the mouth of witnesses: but one witness shall not testify against any person to cause him to die. Moreover ye shall take no satisfaction for the life of a murderer, which is guilty of death: but he shall be surely put to death." (Numbers 35:30-31)* How much clearer can God tells us what price the murderer must pay for his crime? Over and over and over again God repeats the same law and the answer is always the same, but man has become deaf to God's words and laws, and sets up his own laws contrary to God's.

Those laws were not given only for Moses during his time, because if they were only for Moses, then the Ten Commandments do not concern us either. We could say they were for Moses and the Israelites. Should those Commandments have been given only for Moses and the Israelites, then Jesus would not have said: *"Do not think that I came to destroy the Law or the Prophets. I did not come to destroy but to fulfil." (Matthew 5:17)* If we still adhere to the Ten Commandments, then why not adhere to the rest of God's laws. One law is as good as the other which God gave us.

God says: *"So these things shall be for a statute of judgement unto you throughout your generations in all your dwellings." (Numbers 35:29)* God gave us the laws "throughout your generations." God did not give His law and tell Moses that it was for his generation only, but in plural we read generations, which also includes us, because Christ did not come to destroy the law, He came to fulfil it. Whose will was it that gave us all these rules, regulations or Commandments? Of course it was and still is God's will.

Because man does not abide by God's law and God's will, for that reason we have so much crime around us today. The law breakers know that their punishment is small, the penalty means nothing to them, so they start with a small crime and work their way up until they take someone's life. Mankind today is searching for answers from all kinds of people; professors, physiologists, politicians, judges, psychiatrists, and can't find an answer to this problem. During all this time, man forgets to turn to God and look for answers at His laws to fulfil them.

We have read in a number of books from the Bible for the penalty for murderers. Let us continue to look at the Bible and see if there be any more of the same. *"At the mouth of two witnesses, or three witnesses, shall he that is worthy of death be put to death: but at the mouth of one witness he shall not be put to death. The hands of the witnesses shall be first upon him to put him to death, and after ward the hands of all the people. So thou shalt put the evil away from among you." (Deuteronomy 17:6-7)* By whose will? Each and every time, we see God is repeating the same sentence for murderers. God says that one witness is not enough to condemn someone to death, but two or more witnesses are needed, but still the penalty is the same - death to a murderer. God says to put a murderer to death in order to, "put the evil away from among you."

In today's world around us we see so much crime and law breaking. The Holy Bible is filled with laws for everything. A person goes on a drinking spree, causes a car accident and someone is killed. Someone may be drunk and go into someone's home and kill people there. He gets the same treatment as the prisoner who broke into a home and robbed people, the only difference is one will be in the prison for two years and the murderer for 15 years or whatever.

What about those that waste their time in drinking, laziness and eating only, is there any law for such? In the Bible we read Apostle Paul's letter to the Ephesians where he says: *"And be not drunk with wine, wherein is excess, but be filled with the Spirit." (Ephesians 5:18)* Christ made wine from water at the wedding in Canaan, (John 2:1-11), so people would drink, but not to get drunk. What then is one to do with those who do not obey their parents, spend time in gluttony and drinking? God says thus: *"If a man have a stubborn and rebellious son, which will not obey the voice of his father or the voice of his mother, and that when they have chastened him, will not hearken unto them: Then shall his father and his mother lay hold on him, and bring him unto the elders of his city, and unto the gate of his place: And they shall say unto the elders of his city, This our son is stubborn and rebellious, he will not obey our voice: he is glutton, and a drunkard. And all the men of his city shall stone him with stones, that he die: so shalt thou put away evil from among you: And all Israel shall hear and fear." (Deuteronomy 21:18-21)*

Tough, really tough someone may say, but that is what God says to do. That is His will. What else is one supposed to do with a person who does nothing, but spends his families every penny only to eat and drink and as the Bible says: "he is a glutton and a drunkard." God says that such a person should die. Well what kind of crime did he commit? We read previously that if you do not obey your parents, curse them or whatever, the penalty is death. Here God again clearly tells us that such a person must be put to death. Of what good is such a person to his family, community or country?

Another very serious thing that has occurred in the twentieth century is no respect for God's Sabbath or holy day. In the olden days and until about the 1940's no one was ever allowed to do any work on Sunday or a Holy Day - a Sabbath. Look around you today. Listen to the radio or TV on the weekend. The announcers say that it will be a good weekend to work in the garden or the lawn. So what do we see being done on God's Holy Day? If they are not working out in the field, then they are busy working around the yard. They cut the lawn, paint fences or houses, washing clothes, doing all kinds of work in and around the yard and house. What is God's will about working on His Holy Day? God says: *"Six days shall work be done, but on the seventh day, a Sabbath or rest to the Lord: Whosoever does work therein shall be put to death." (Exodus 35:2)*

W H A T ? What a serious punishment people will say. But that is God's will. How many people have we seen that were put to death for working on a Sunday, Holy Day, Sabbath? When and to whom did God say to throw out that law? Jesus Himself said that He came to fulfil the law. The problem is that today man has made himself a god, and no one can tell him anything. Excuses, excuses, excuses. *"Whosoever does work therein, shall be put to death." (Exodus 35:2)*

It is all God's will. He does everything, as previously said, good and bad. *"The Lord kills , and makes alive; He brings down to the grave, and brings up. The Lord make poor, and makes rich: He brings low and lifts up; He raises up the poor out of the dust, and lifts up the beggar from the dunghill." (I Samuel 2:6-8)* The Lord can do all those things and everything else. By His will He can do what we can never even think of. In today's modern and technological world that we have around us, it has become so grave because God has willed it to happen. He could have prevented man from inventing the telephone, the computer, TV, refrigerator and everything else, by not granting man the wisdom to invent such conveniences. God in His goodness gave man the knowledge to invent all kinds of things for his convenience. Instead of thanking God, for those inventions, man made himself god, and threw God out of his life.

Who makes some people rich and others poor? Why are the people so well off in North America while in the third world countries, thousands die each day due to lack of food? Who makes that some people have homes like palaces and others are homeless sleeping in the back lanes of cities or under trees, bridges, and in cardboard boxes? Who gives to some people so much food that they discard much of it into the waste while others die of starvation? Who gives to some people clothing, that they do not know what to wear each day, while others have rags hanging on their backs or nothing at all? God makes everything good and evil by His will. *"The Lord hath made all things for Himself: Yea, even the wicked for the days of evil." (Proverbs 16:4)*

As mentioned previously a number of times, everything is

made by Gods will. You go to work in the morning, but know not, if by God's will you will return back home to your family that day. In November 1999 a plane of Egypt Air, with 217 people abroad crashed into the ocean of the east coast of USA. Had those people known that would happen, do you think anyone would have boarded that plane that day? By whose will did that plane crash and many others previous to and since then? Was it the will of the captain of the plane? Was it the mechanic on the ground? Was it one of the passengers? God's will does everything around us each and every day. God's will is stronger than the will of all the people of this world put together. All the people on earth want to live in luxury and live forever, but God's will is that we all will perish for not obeying Him. With one thought God wiped every living thing off the face of the earth, except Noah, his family and two of all creatures.

Every person on earth loves some things and hates other things. There are things you love and wish to have all the time, family, wealth, pleasure, etc., while at other times there are things you never wish to have, illness, misfortune, grief, sorrow, heartache..... If man can love and hate, what about God? Does He only love, or does He also hate? God loved and hated things before we did. He loved the world and all that He created upon it. *"And God saw everything that He made, and, behold, it was very good." (Genesis 1:31)*

God made the world and He made it good. He loved it, but later He repented and was sorry that He created man on earth. *"And God saw the wickedness of man was great in the earth, and that every imagination of his was only evil continually. And it repented the Lord that He had made man on earth, and it grieved Him at His heart. And the Lord said; I will destroy man whom I have created from the face of the earth; both man, and beast, and the creeping thing, and the fowls of the air: for it repents Me that I have made them."(Genesis 6:5-7)* God destroyed everything beside Noah and what was in the ark. God thought, that following Noah, man would be different and God would be pleased with him, but man has again become as sinful as it was during the time of Noah and is doing the same thing again. *"And as it was in the days of Noah, so shall it be also in the days of the Son of man." (Luke 17:26)* What alternative will God have to do with this sinful world, if not to destroy it again? By whose will?

When someone does something wrong, they get punished for it. It is the same with God. When we step out of line, we must get punished for our wrongdoings. By His will, He punishes us and will continue to punish man until man comes to his senses and changes his way, or until God will destroy him.

The Bible is filled with laws of how God wants man to live to have everlasting life. God made laws like today man is making all kinds of his own laws, many different and opposite to God's. Man has made laws, to stop at stop signs and red lights, to pay taxes, children must attend school, work only eight hours a day, set a minimum wage, etc. But God's laws are greater than man's laws. If we break man's laws, we are given a light sentence of punishment, if any. I do not call probation or a suspended sentence as any kind of punishment for a crime. When God punishes, it hurts, because He can punish us in different ways and the worst is spiritual death, a separation from God for eternity. God abhors the breaking of His laws and says that it is an abomination. And by whose will?

Man thinks that he has made wise laws concerning life. But what does God say about such laws? *"For My thoughts are not your thoughts, neither are you ways My ways, saith the Lord. For as the heavens are higher than the earth, so are My ways higher than your ways, and My thoughts than your thoughts."* (Isaiah 55:8-9)

Abhor and abomination are similar in meaning as the Webster dictionary says: Abhor: to hate extremely, to detest, to be opposed.

Abomination: extreme hatred, detestation, defilement. Now that we see the two words are similar, what does God say how He feels about breaking His laws? All His abominations are not being listed here, but one only needs to read the Book of Leviticus, and we can find everything one needs to know how to live on this earth by God's laws.

Every time we turn in whichever direction, all we hear is about rights. Human rights, civil rights, womens rights, workers rights, etc. But has anyone ever stopped to think what about GOD'S RIGHTS? Does God not have any rights at all? He is the one who created everything, isn't He? Does God not have any more rights to what He created? He had created everything good as we read a few paragraphs back? But man has polluted the goodness that God had created. Turn to the Bible and there you will see all God's rights. The problem is that man has thrown out God's rights and substituted his own in place. Man's rights cannot be equalled or even compared to God's rights. His rights are the right ways since the creation of the world.

Man makes one law today and tomorrow he changes it. In Canada and the USA the two countries were established on the laws of Christianity because those are the only true and right laws. Today in these countries, many, many of God's laws based on Christian values have been thrown out, ignored or changed into man's own laws which he likes. Is God in agreement, and does He like the laws man has made? Again some will stand and protest that what happened in the Old Testament is not good for the Christians and present times, because Jesus came down and everything is different. Have I not mentioned already that Jesus Himself said: *"Think not that I come to destroy the law, or the prophets: I am come not to destroy, but to fulfil." (Matthew 5:17)* Nowhere did Jesus ever mention or say that He came to throw out or change the laws that God had set. Nowhere did He tell us to throw God's laws out and set our own. He came to fulfil what His and our Father created and established and by whose will?

In the book of Leviticus laws are found about adultery, bestiality, etc. Today some churches have even opened their doors to bring pets and animals to church to have them blessed. Some churches have opened their doors to prostitutes to bring them into the church to give them food. What does God say about all this? What is His will on this matter? *"Thou shalt not bring the hire of a whore, or the price of a dog into the house of the Lord thy God for any vow: for even both these are abomination unto the Lord thy God." (Deuteronomy 23:18)* All laws written in the Bible are by God's will.

We know what a dreadful disease leprosy is. God even gave laws regarding leprosy, saying: *"Take heed in the plague of leprosy, that thou observe diligently, and do according to all that the priests the Levites shall teach you: As I commanded them, so ye shall observe to do." (Deuteronomy 24:8)* No one would ever want to get inflicted with such a disease. Leprosy or for that matter any other illness or sickness comes to man by God's will. In the New Bible Commentary by Davidson, Stubbs and Kevan, we read regarding leprosy and God's will: "Every wilderness experience was to be regarded as a lesson illustrating God's will and purpose for His people." (Page 216)

We know from the New Testament that Jesus came to Jerusalem one day where there is a pool called, "Bethesda." There Jesus found a man who had been paralysed for 38 years, a cripple who could not walk. Jesus made him well and later found the man in the temple. Maybe he had gone to the temple to thank God for being healed, but Jesus said to him: *"Behold thou art made whole: sin no more, lest a worse thing come unto thee." (John 5:14)* What could be worse then being paralysed and helpless for thirty-eight years? Yet something worse could come, separation from God for eternity. Here Jesus tells the man not to sin, so worst things don't come to him. Jesus ties sin to punishment. That is exactly what has been said all along. People should obey God's laws so something worse does not come to them. By breaking God's laws, one commits sin and for sin Christ says something worst could happen. What does the Scripture say about the penalty for sin? *"For the wages of sin is death; but the gift of God is eternal life through Jesus Christ our Lord." (Romans 6:23)*

Another abomination for God is the wearing of garments-clothing. Today people have no sense of right from wrong. People put on and wear whatever they think that looks good on them. God tells us what we should wear, saying: *"The woman shall not wear that which pertains unto a man, neither shall a man put on a woman's garment: for all that do so are abomination unto the Lord thy God." (Deuteronomy 22:5)* Look around you. Look at the TV programs. Look in the newspaper. What do you see? Sometimes you can't tell if one is a man or woman the way they dress and what they do. Look at their clothing, look at their hairdos, look at the rings on their hands. Look at the trinkets stuck in their ears, nose, eyelids, cheeks or other body parts. When we lived on the farm, people put rings into the noses of bulls and boars to hold them. Today people put rings in their noses. Is that human? Is that from well thinking people? Even animals don't do what some people do. Is that natural? By no means - no.

When the prodigal son spent all the wealth his father had given him, he repented for his wrong and returned back home. When his father saw him, he rejoiced, and said: *"Bring forth the best robe, and put it on him: and put a ring on his hand, and shoes on his feet." (Luke 15:22)* The father said to put the ring on his hand, not in the nose, the ear, eyelids, etc. Today man has made a mockery of himself by putting rings in places were they never belonged and don't belong. What is this world coming to anyway? The proverbs say: *"As a jewel of gold in a swine's snout, so is a fair woman which is without discretion." (Proverbs 11:22)* A ring in a swine's snout. What has man become with rings in his nose? Man is bringing himself and this world to destruction. One day God will not be able to tolerate all the nonsense and ignorance of man and will have no choice left, but to destroy this world as He did during Noah's time. By His will He will destroy the world.

This second destruction will not be by flood, for God made a promise never again to destroy the world by deluge. *"And I will establish My covenant with you: neither shall all flesh be cut off any more by the waters of a flood: neither shall there anymore be a flood to destroy the earth. And God said, This is the token of the covenant which I make between Me and you and every living creature that is with you, for perpetual generations: I do set my bow in the cloud, and it shall be a token of a covenant between Me and the earth. And it shall come to pass, when I bring a cloud over the earth, that the bow shall be seen in the cloud: And I will remember My covenant, which is between Me and you and every living creature of all flesh; and the waters shall no more become a flood to destroy all flesh. And the bow shall be in the cloud; and I will look upon it, that I may remember the everlasting covenant between God and every living creature of all flesh that is upon the earth." (Genesis 9:11-16)* God has kept that promise to this very day. He has not and will not destroy the world again by a flood and His promise is the bow (rainbow) in the sky to show us from time to time to remember His promise. But does man know who God is and obeys his Creator?

If man does not change his ways of living very soon, to follow God's laws, not his own, God will have no choice left but to destroy this earth again. Only the destruction will, not come by a deluge, but by fire. *"But the heavens and the earth, which are now, by the same word are kept in store, reserved unto fire against the day of judgement and perdition of ungodly men." (II Peter 3:7)* Peter also says similar words: *"Looking for and hasting unto the coming of the day of God, wherein the heavens being on fire shall be dissolved, and the elements shall melt with fervent heat." (II Peter 3:12)* It is scary, but Peter tells us more: *"But the day of the Lord will come as a thief in the night; in the which the heavens shall pass away with a great noise, and the elements shall melt with fervent heat, the earth also and the works that are therein shall be burned up." (II Peter 3:10)*

Reading such things and knowing what God has in store for this world, what should we do? Will we be able to hide anywhere? No, it will be the end of everything. Everything will be consumed in fire. The only thing man can do today, before the judgement day comes, is to make a "turn about" 180 degrees, and start to live by God's laws. Follow His commandments. Read what the Bible says. Get rid of all the nonsense that man has invented and live as God wants us to, or else we all will face the consequences that He has in store for us if we don't change and repent.

In the prophetical Book of Revelations we also read of similar events of the fire destroying the earth. *"The first Angel sounded, and there followed hail and fire mingled with blood, and they were cast upon the earth: and the third part of the trees was burnt up, and all the green grass was burnt up." (Revelations 8:7)* The two chapters of Revelations eight and nine, tell us of the seven Angels each doing their part by the will of God, to bring down fire upon the earth and destroy it.

The Good Book tells us of many other things that God hates. I will only mention a few. All of the things that God hates can be read in the Bible. *"Six things doth the Lord hate: yea, seven are an abomination unto Him. A proud look, a lying tongue, and hands that shed innocent blood. A heart that devises, wicked imaginations, feet that be swift in running to mischief, a false witness that speaks lies, and he that sows discord among brethren." (Proverbs 6:16-19)*

Another place in the Scriptures where we see suffering and pain come upon the people by God's will is: *"But if ye will not hearken unto Me, and will not do all these commandments: And if ye shall despise My statutes, or if your soul abhor My judgements, so that ye will not do all My commandments, but that ye break My* covenant: I also will do this unto you: I will even appoint over you terror, consumption, and the burning ague, that shall consume the eyes, and cause sorrow of heart: and ye shall sow your seed in vain, for your enemies shall eat it. And I will set My face against you, and ye shall be slain before your enemies: they that hate you shall reign over you: and ye shall flee when non pursues you. And if ye will not yet for all this hearken unto Me, then I will punish you seven times more for your sins." (Leviticus 26:14-18)* Are those not the words of God that He will punish sinners? If we say that God is good, why than does He say that He will punish us seven times more for our sins? And He will punish man by whose will?

What does Apostle Paul say about people doing evil, sinning? *"Abhor that which is evil." (Romans 12:9)* So much evil in the world around us today and Apostle Paul says: *"Be not overcome of evil, but overcome evil with good." (Romans 12:21)* God gave us good laws, why do we not abide by them, but make our own laws? Yes there are still people that do well or try to do well, but at the same time there are those that do evil also. Today there are more evil doers then those that do good. We hear so little today about good being done. Each time you turn on the TV or radio, all you can hear is evil and bad, murders, robberies, home invasions, shootings, fighting, assaults, drive-by shootings, etc. All of these things, plus the good things come by God's will. *"Therefore it shall come to pass, that as all good things are come upon you, which the Lord your God promised you: so shall the Lord bring upon you all evil things, until He has destroyed you from off this good land which the Lord your God hath given you." (Joshua 23:15).*

If we live with God, in other words, by God's commandments, to follow and obey Him, He will send His blessings upon us. If we live without God and make other things as our gods or even make ourselves as a god, then He will have no choice but by His will to come, punish and destroy us as He mentions so many times which we read in the Holy Scriptures. *"And I will bring a sword upon you, that shall avenge the quarrel of My covenant: and when ye are gathered together within your cities, I will send the pestilence among you; and ye shall be delivered into the hand of the enemy."* (Leviticus 26:25) *"Then I will walk contrary unto you also in fury; and I, even I, will chastise you seven times for your sins."*(Leviticus 26:28) *"When ye have transgressed the covenant of the Lord your God, which He commanded you, and have gone and served other gods, and bowed yourselves to them; then shall the anger of the Lord be kindled against you, and ye shall perish quickly from off the good land which He hath given unto you."* (Joshua 23:16)

Man today has taken to himself other gods such as; wealth, pleasure, politics, idols, sex, sports, etc. Man puts more time into pleasure, drinking, gambling, good times, then he ever thinks about God and what God has in store for him if he does not change his ways. *"I will early destroy all the wicked of the land; that I may cut off all wicked doers from the city of the Lord."* (Psalm 101:8) *"Behold, the day of the Lord comes, cruel both with wrath and fierce anger, to lay the land desolate: and He shall destroy the sinners thereof out of it."* (Isaiah 13:9) *"Behold, therefore I will stretch out mine hand upon thee, and will deliver thee for a spoil to the heathen; and I will cause thee to perish out of the countries: I will destroy thee: and thou shalt know that I am the Lord."* (Ezekiel 25:7) This above will be done by God's will.

These are places from the Scriptures where we learn that God had destroyed man before, destroys him today and will destroy him in the future because of man's sins. Today we still have the same God in heaven that was in the Old Testament times. He has not changed. His laws are still the same for all humanity. The time has come for man to repent, to change and come closer to God and live with Him.

A very disgraceful thing we see today in and around us, is the younger men growing long hair and beards. Even some clergy have gone the same route and then tie their hair up into a pony tail. What does the Bible say on this subject and about the priests dress code? Ezekiel chapter 44 gives ordinances for priests. Plainly it states that when a priest has put on vestments or robes of service, he cannot go among the people unless he takes his vestments off. As for long or short hair we read: *"Neither shall they shave their heads, nor suffer their locks to grow long, they shall only poll their heads. (Ezekiel 44:20)* "Nor suffer their locks to grow long" says the Old Testament. In the New Testament Apostle Paul writes to the Corinthians saying: *"Doth not even nature itself teach you, that, if a man have long hair, it is a shame unto him?" (I Corinthians 11:14)* At the same time he speaks about women and their head saying: *"But if a woman have long hair, it is a glory to her: for her hair is given her for a covering." (I Corinthians 11:15)* By whose will are the above words written? By the Apostles with the Holy Spirit influence. And the Holy Spirit is the third person of the Holy trinity and the Holy Trinity is God, so the above words are written for us by God's will. Today it seems like the world has turned upside down. Younger men are wearing longer hair and many women are cutting their hair shorter and some are even shaving their heads. These things are being done in opposition to what the words in the Scriptures tell us.

On the subject of hair, what about going to church for prayers, how does one dress their head? Apostle Paul says this:*"Every man praying or prophesying having his head covered, dishonours his head. But every woman that prays or prophesying with her head uncovered dishonours her head: for that is even all one as if she were shaven. For if the woman be not covered, let her also be shorn: but if it be a shame for a woman to be shorn or shaven, let her be covered. For a man in deed ought not to cover his head, for as much as he is the image and glory of God: but the woman is the glory of the man." (I Corinthians 11:4-7)* This is a very clear and simple explanation as how one ought to go to church for any kind of prayer, men with head's uncovered and women with heads covered. No one can now say that this is Old Testament rules. This was written by Apostle Paul as he learned from Christ, other apostles and disciples.

Today there are still many people in the twenty-first century who still say: "That is not written anywhere in the Bible, why do we have to do that?" But is everything people do in their homes, churches, at work, written in the Bible? Evangelist John tells us the closing words in his Gospel thus: *"And there are also many other things which Jesus did, the which if they should be written everyone, I suppose that even the world itself could not contain the books that should be written. Amen." (John 21:25)*

So everything that was done and said is not written in the Holy Books. The main things that God wanted us to know and believe, are in the Bible. By His will are things done and what He willed, it was written for our benefit. The other things we have in the churches is called, "Holy tradition." It is something that is passed on from person to person by mouth. If a mother wants to teach her daughter how to do some things, does she write everything down? If she lives to be seventy-five years old and she had to write every word down for her daughter, how many books would she need to write. Can you imagine how many books it would take if all the mothers that ever lived wrote every word down for their daughters? Where would they put all those books? That is why everything that Jesus did is not in the Bible, but is being passed down as we say by Holy Tradition from generation to generation. That is why we have many of the things in the church that Jesus did but was not written down and found in the Bible. Maybe the Apostles and Evangelists would have wanted to write everything down, but they could not because their life on earth ran out.

They were all martyred and could not write everything down as they may have wanted to. They did not have computers and printing presses to write everything down. They did not have paper like we have today, to have put everything down. So we have many things that were done by Christ and His Apostles, but some of those things are not written down and we know them as Holy Tradition.

I am sure that some people and maybe even you yourself from time to time got angry at someone or something. This brings pain to them and to God. Some may protest and say that God does not get angry because He is a God and is merciful, good, kind, forgiving us our sins. They say that Jesus died on the cross for us, so our sins are forgiven even when we get angry. If and when people repent of their sins, God will also repent of His anger toward the people.

In the Bible we read: *"And there shall cleave not of the cursed thing to thine hand: that the Lord may turn from the fierceness of His anger, and shew thee mercy, and have compassion upon thee, and multiply thee, as He hath sworn unto thy fathers." (Deuteronomy 13:17)* We also read in the Book of Job: *"If God will not withdraw His anger, the proud helpers do stoop under Him." (Job 9:13)* Jesus the Son of God also was angry at times when people did not listen to Him. One day in the temple He healed a man with a withered hand. The people began to complain against Him for healing the man on the Sabbath day. We read in the Scriptures: *"And when He had looked round about on them with anger, being grieved for the hardness of their hearts, He said to the man, Stretch forth thine hand. And he stretched it out: and his hand was restored as the other." (Mark 3:5)* We see the Bible telling us that Jesus looked at them in anger. So the man's hand was healed, by whose will? By whose will was Jesus angry at the Pharisees?

Let us recall another incident when Jesus went into the temple and overthrew the tables and chased out the money changers out of the temple. *"And Jesus went into the temple of God, and cast out all of them that sold and bought in the temple, and overthrew the tables of the money changers, and the seats of them that sold doves." (Matthew 21:12) (Mark 11:15)* Why did Jesus overthrow the tables? Was it because He was so happy and full of joy? He was angry as the Bible says: *"And said unto them. It is written, My house shall be called the house of prayer; and ye have made it a den of thieves." (Matthew 21:13)*

What about the churches today, are they all houses of prayer, or have we made them into theaters, halls and only sometimes into a house of prayer? Go into some church and see what happens in it. Does it feel like a church? Does it feel like a house of prayer? Can you feel holiness and sanctity in it? I myself have seen churches where people come in and have concerts. They have all kinds of fun, they laugh and joke and have as some would say, "a jolly good time." I have seen some churches where animals were brought into the church to participate in a Christmas and Easter pageants.

In one church where the altar stands, the animal(camel) did what is done when nature calls. Is that a church doing such things? It is a "den of thieves" as Jesus called the people in the temple when He chased them out and overturned the tables. If Jesus should come to such a church today, when a concert or play is going on in that church, would He recognize it as His Fathers house of prayer? When such things happen to God's church (House of Prayer), how long can God suffer such things? How and what should He do to those that dishonour His House of Prayer? Do such people not deserve punishment for such actions? Where is the sanctity in such a church? Where is the religiosity in that church?

One time I had an opportunity to be at a special service in one of the newer churches in the 21st century. As I came in I sat on the right side towards the back of that church. Beside me against the wall, I saw a bunch of drums sitting along the wall. I looked to the front, and on the stage another bunch of drums. Way up above the drums stands a screen for viewing slides or movies. I did not know if I was in some hall or auditorium not in a church.

What will be the next thing in that church? Pews taken out and dancing instituted?

When God punishes us, does He do that because He wants to? Is He happy to do that, and is He full of joy doing that? It is because of God's anger against us for not living by His laws, and what we do with His church. The Scriptures tell us: *"Behold, the day of the Lord comes, cruel both with wrath and fierce anger, to lay the land desolate: and He shall destroy the sinners thereof out of it." (Isaiah 13:9)* Farther it is written again: *"Therefore I will shake the heavens, and the earth shall remove out of her place, in the wrath of the Lord of hosts, and in the day of His fierce anger." (Isaiah 13:13)*

God does not have just any kind of anger against the sinners, but as Isaiah says, "fierce anger." There is more: *"Therefore thus saith the Lord God; Behold, Mine anger and My fury shall be poured out upon this place, upon man, and upon beast, and upon the trees of the field, and upon the fruit of the ground; and it shall burn, and shall not be quenched."(Jeremiah 7:20)* There are many other places mentioned in the Holy Scriptures about God's anger at us. It is true that He is merciful and also forgives us our wrong doings, but only if we repent and obey His laws.

We cannot even begin to compare our anger to God's. When He gets angry, He will send upon us storms, earthquakes, tornadoes, hurricanes, diseases, misfortunes, etc., and we will not be spared by Him. *"The Lord will not spare him, but the anger of the Lord and His jealousy shall smoke against that man, and all the curses that are written in this book shall be upon him, and the Lord shall blot out his name from under heaven." (Deuteronomy 29:20)* This is serious stuff, and God will not play lightly with sinners. In the same chapter we read: *"Even all nations shall say, wherefore hath the Lord done thus unto this land? What means the heat of this great anger?" (Deuteronomy 29:24).* People will ask and wonder why God will be doing such things against man. The answer is, that man has angered God with his sinful life on earth and at the same time forgetting God and bringing God's curse on himself. Further on we read: *"And the anger of the Lord was kindled against this land, to bring upon it all the curses that are written in this book: and the Lord rooted them out of their land in anger, and in wrath, and in great indignation, and cast them into another land, as it is to this day." (Deuteronomy 29:27-28)*

So, we see that there is anger in the Lord too. Many churches today do not teach any of these things because they don't like it. They only teach about the goodness of God, but why don't they also mention and talk what God will and can do when He gets angry over our ways for not obeying Him. We heard what happened in the temple when Jesus came and the temple had been turned into a "den of thieves." As mentioned above, what do we see happening in many of today's churches? If Jesus came today to a service, wedding or a funeral being held in a church, would He recognize it as His church? Would He be happy? Would His heart be saddened? Would He be angry? Would He also chase the people out and ask what has been done with His Father's house of prayer?

Open your eyes and ears next time you go into any church. Is it peaceful and quiet? Can you pray there before the service starts? Is the atmosphere prayerful before and after the service? Or at a wedding before the service starts you will hear people talking, laughing. When the bride and groom leave the church, people do the same thing- laugh, clap, etc. People clap and whistle when the bride and groom are introduced as Mr. And Mrs. The inside of the church before and after the marriage service starts, does not seem like a church. It sounds more like some open-air market. Everyone is trying to out talk everyone else. Everyone seems to be talking to the people in front of them, to their side and the ones behind all at the same time. Really next time just stop and look how many are really praying before the service starts.

Where everyone should be meditating and praying before the service starts, praying for the bride and groom before they come to get married, praying for the deceased whose body is lying in the church, the people talk about gardens, and tillers, and cars and tractors, and cows and horses, and kitchens and bathrooms, and everything else that comes to their mind under the sun. I believe that if Jesus walked into a church before the bride and groom come in and stood in the corner, watched and listened, He would not recognize it as His Father's house.

On January 7, 1999, as I was coming from my fathers place, Cudworth, Saskatchewan, on the way home to Calgary with my late wife, we turned on the radio from one of the stations in Calgary. The announcer said that he will be having an interview with a bishop in one church in Hawaii. A few minutes later their conversation began as he contacted the bishop in this prominent church. He asked the bishop a few things about the church, then his congregation and then the announcer put a question to the bishop. The conversation went something like this."Your excellency, is it true that during the service in your church you have Hawaiian hula dancers doing the Hawaiian dances?" The bishop replied that it's true but they do not dance during the Lord's Prayer and during communion. The announcer asks him another question: "Your excellency, do I understand correctly that when the Hawaiian dance is done, the women dance with bare breasts?" The bishop replied that it is correct. Now just think for a moment: If Jesus walked into that church during that service, would He recognize it as His church which He established some 2000 years ago? Would He think that it is some theater or hall? What have God's Prayer Houses become today? Would Christ also grab such people and throw them all unto the street? Right now God's will is beginning to think of what action God should take against the sinners of His land.

People come to church to pray. Why then do they have to talk with their friends or neighbours about everything under the sun, instead of praying while in church?

What does a new planted lawn have to do with prayer when we talk about it to our friends in church? Pray and thank God that you planted the lawn, thank Him that it began to grow, ask Him that it be a healthy and good lawn, but why talk in church about all kinds of things but God? The church is a place to talk to, with and about God. People come to church to petition or ask God for things. People come to thank God for all the benefits that they receive from God. People come to glorify God and to ask for mercy for their sins. That is what a church is for and all about. How can someone concentrate and pray when you feel and hear as though you are in an outside open air market, or at some sports spectacle? When you come to church, come to pray and if you have to tell someone something, phone them at home. Everyone has a telephone. Better yet, go over to someone's place and visit them and tell them all you have to say, but leave the church be a church and a "House of Prayer."

Remember that the church is different than a house, a store, a garage, bar, etc. What you do in a barn, you don't do in the house. What you do in the house, you do not do in a garage. What you do in a store, you don't do at home. People should learn that when they go to church they should not talk about their golf game, or how many fish they caught, or how much garden they planted. When in church pray. If you must say the same prayer fifteen times, one for each person for their health, a safe journey or whatever, then do it.

The thing is, will you be able to pray if people in front of you, behind and on your side will keep gabbing away about everything under the sun. Do you think that because you come to church and the louder and more you talk, that God will hear you better then your neighbour? Come to church and pray, don't speak as Matthew tells us. *"But when ye pray, use not vain repetitions, as the heathen do; for they think that they shall be heard for their much speaking."(Matthew 6:7)* You don't have to speak much, just speak wisely with God in your thoughts. Take a few moments when in church and direct your thoughts to God. Take those few moments to be alone with God.

I say, maybe sometimes there is a person who came to pray and be with God, but the noise the other people make, just throws the person of and they can't concentrate and pray. The next time when the service is held that person may not come to church because they will say they can't pray in such an atmosphere. All week long you were over burdened with all kinds of work, all kinds of thoughts, all kinds of distractions and when Sunday comes, you should focus your thoughts on prayer to God. Come Sunday morning, take a few moments of time in peace and quiet and pray to God instead of talking to your friends before the service. Give that time of peace and quietness to God, it is His day, like the Scripture says: *"Render therefore unto Caesar the things which are Caesar's; and unto God the things that are God's." (Matthew 22:21) (Mark 12:17)*

Another question that could be asked at this time is: Why do you go to church? The first thing that the person would answer would probably be - to pray. To pray for whom and for what? We come to church to glorify God, to worship Him, to request or petition Him for things for ourselves and for others, to thank Him for everything and in the end to fulfil HIS WILL. We can pray and ask God for health for ourselves and for others who may be ill. Pray for good weather. Pray for the prisoners. Pray for those that are on some journey. Pray for those that must be at work, doctors, nurses, firemen, policemen, because of their work they can't be in church. Pray all the time and not only in church, but the church is the best place to pray. But always pray. *"And He spoke a parable unto them to this end, that men ought always to pray, and not to faint." (Luke 18:1) "Pray without ceasing."* says

Apostle Paul in *(I Thessalonians 5:17) "For this cause we also, since the day we heard it, do not cease to pray for you, and to desire that ye might be filled with the knowledge of His will in all wisdom and spiritual understanding." (Colossians 1:9)* There are many other places mentioned in the Bible to pray.

People live in neighbourhoods and at times things happen that people become enemies. In such a case what do people do? Some don't want to meet their neighbour. Others take matters to court. Others may cause some harm or injury to their neighbour, etc. What did Jesus say to do with enemies? *"But I say unto you, Love your enemies, bless them that curse you, do well to them that hate you, and pray for them which despitefully use you and persecute you." (Matthew 5:44) "Bless them which persecute you, bless and curse not." (Romans 12:14)* Instead of praying for their enemies, people swear and curse them and that is not what Jesus and the church teach.

All things being done on earth and heaven are of God's will as has already been mentioned over and over again. It should be stressed more each time that it is God Who controls the sun, wind, rain, etc. Everything comes from Him by His will. *"And all the inhabitants of the earth are reputed as nothing: and He does according to His will in the army of heaven, and among the inhabitants of the earth: and none can stay His hand or say unto Him. What does Thou?" (Daniel 4:35)* As it says, He does according to His will in things in heaven and people on earth and we can't say or do anything about it. No one can stop a flood, hurricane, tornado, earthquake, etc., because His will is stronger and He does as He wills. Everything and all things are of God. *"And all things are of God, Who hath reconciled us to Himself by Jesus Christ, and hath given to us the ministering of reconciliation." (II Corinthians 5:18)*

Are you content with what you are and what you have? If not, why not? Is it not God's will that all you have comes from

Him to you by His will? Apostle Paul writes in his letter to the Hebrews: *"Let your conversation be without covetousness; and be content with such things as ye have: for He hath said, I will never leave thee, nor forsake thee." (Hebrews 13:5)* Writing in his letter to the Philippians Apostle Paul tells them the same thing. *"Not that I speak in respect of want: for I have learned, in whatsoever state I am, therewith to be content." (Philippians 4:11)* Yes there are many people on earth that they will never be satisfied and content, no matter what and how much they have. No matter how much more they have then someone else, they are never content. There is a saying: "The more they have, the more they want." People have homes, a few automobiles in their yard, conveniences, jobs, etc., and yet they are not content or satisfied. Why not? Because they want more. Are the people in Africa, Serbia, Yugoslavia or the third world countries better off then you? So why is the western world always complaining and always looking for more and more? Why do we always want to have more then the next person? Did Christ have more than others? What did He say about Himself? *"The foxes have holes, and the birds of the air have nests; but the Son of man hath not where to lay His Head." (Matthew 8:20)(Luke 9:58)* Christ did not have a car, nor a house after He left His Mother Mary.

Do you think you will take everything with you to the other world? When will you be content if you are not content today with what you have? Is it not a sin to complain that we have so much while others have nothing in many countries? When the Israelites journeyed to Paran they rested and camped and one day they began to complain. What did God say to the complainers? *"And when the people complained, it displeased the Lord: and the Lord heard it; and His anger was kindled; and the fire of the Lord burnt among them, and consumed them that were in the uttermost parts of the camp." (Numbers 11:1)*

Do people complain because they are greedy, selfish and they always want to have more than their neighbour? A relative of Jesus, Jude, writes in his only letter in the New Testament thus: *"And Enoch also, the seventh from Adam, prophesied of these sayings: Behold, the Lord comes with ten thousand of His saints, to execute judgement upon all, and to convince all that are ungodly among them all their ungodly deeds which they have ungodly committed, and all their hard speeches which ungodly sinners have spoken against Him. These are murmurers, complainers, walking after their own lusts; and their mouth speaks great swelling words, having mens persons in admiration because of advantage." (Jude 14-16)*

Jude says that the murmurers and complainers look after their own lusts, their own pleasures to satisfy themselves. After the complainers, strikers received a higher salary, did they give anymore or anything of that or at all to those that have less? How much of the higher wages did they give to the blind, the homeless, the crippled, aged, etc.

Most people today forget, don't know, or don't want to know what the Holy Scripture says. We read: *"I have showed you all things, how that labouring ye ought to support the weak, and to remember the words of the Lord Jesus, how He said, It is more blessed to give then to receive." (Acts 20:35)* How many times have you seen the strikers, complainers, murmurers go out on strike, get more money and are they satisfied? No, for in a very short while, and they start complaining again and once again go out on strike and leave many people suffering on account of them. I still have to see someone who has a job that they are starving to death in this country. If people only followed God's laws, live by them, there would never be any wars, misunderstandings, grumbling, dissatisfaction etc. But no matter how much you give for someone they will never be satisfied. Can the strikers and complainers set a law and say when enough is going to be enough? Why can't we never hear someone say, give us this much and we will never ask for anything more again. We never hear this, but only give more, give more and give more. When will enough be enough? And what was the salary that Jesus got for being a teacher, doctor, friend, etc. Yes He got paid. How? By being Crucified.

Did you thank God for all that He has given you? So God has given you the health, strength, energy, wisdom to acquire what you have, but how much have you given back in return to God? How much do you think you should give? Yes, God told us how much we should give to Him. When I say to give to God, that means to the church, the homeless, blind, crippled, etc. God told us that we should give ten percent of our income. Is that how much you gave last year, the whole ten percent? Was it really ten percent, or half of ten, or a tenth of tenth or nothing? That was your will if you gave anything, but how about God's will to give Him ten percent?

Tithing or ten percent goes a way back to the Old Testament to the very first book in the Bible where we read: *"And blessed be the Most High God, which hath delivered thine enemies into thy hand. And he gave Him tithes." (Genesis 14:20)* Farther on we read again: *"And all the tithe of the land, whether of the seed of the land, or the fruit of the tree, is the Lord's; it is holy unto the Lord." (Leviticus 27:30)* If everyone gave a tithe of his yearly income, there would be no need going around begging from house to house, in the church, organizations, clubs, etc., because there would be enough funds to go around for all the homeless, crippled, blind, deaf, etc. Tithing is giving ten percent of your yearly income. Is that how much you gave last year? It's not the priest or the church that set a tithing law, but God, and if you are a God-fearing person, than you should obey as God says to do.

Not only in the Old Testament do we see tithing, but Jesus also taught about tithing. Jesus told us the story of the two men that went to the temple to pray, a Pharisee and a publican. The Pharisee stood in the middle of the church boasting, so everyone would see and hear him as he said: *"I fast twice in the week, I give tithes of all I possess.*" *(Luke 18:12)* We also see in the New Testament Christ scolding the Pharisees and the scribes about their tithing: "*Woe unto you, scribes and Pharisees, hypocrites! For you pay tithe of mint and anise and cummin, and have omitted the weightier matters of the law, judgement, mercy, and faith: these ought ye to have done, and not leave the other undone.*" *(Matthew 23:23)* Here Christ mentions that their tithes are in goods, but what kind, when at the same time they forget about mercy, faith, etc. Previously I mentioned about our judgement day (Matthew 25:31-46), that we will be judged on how we helped the hungry, naked, thirsty, sick, etc. "*And, behold, I have given the children of Levi all the tenth in Israel for an inheritance, for their service which they serve, even the service of the tabernacle of the congregation.*" *(Numbers 18:21)* As the Old Testament was coming to the close and a new era was approaching, we again see tithing mentioned. "*Will a man rob God? Yet ye have robbed Me. But ye say, Wherein have we robbed Thee? In tithes and offerings.*" *(Malach 3:8)*

By God's commandment and will the priests have the right to take tithes. "*And verily they that are the sons of Levi, who receive the office of the priesthood, have a commandment to take tithes of the people according to the law, that is, of their brethren, though they come out of the loins of Abraham.*" *(Hebrews 7:5)* (See Numbers 18:21 above)

As we see by God's commandment and law, we should be giving a tithe (ten percent) of all our income. What a glorious day that would be for the churches of God and also for those who give a tithe, for in return God will reward that person a hundredfold, a hundred times more for giving gifts, gifts of yearly income from each person. We should give until like the saying says: "Give until it hurts." "*And everyone that hath forsaken house, or brethren, or sister, or father, or mother, or wife, or children, or lands for My Name's sake, shall receive a hundredfold, and shall inherit everlasting life.*"*(Matthew 19:29)* Where do you want to live, here on earth and enjoy a few years of goods or to live with God in everlasting life?

We must always remember that whatever we do, we should do for the glory of God. By doing so, He will bless us and fulfil our dreams and wishes as He Himself said: *"Ask, and it shall be given you: seek and ye shall find: knock and it shall be opened unto you."* *(Matthew 7:7)* Jesus also said to ask Him and His Father for things in our prayers. *"And all things whatsoever ye shall ask in prayer, believing, ye shall receive."* *(Matthew 21:22)* Jesus plainly tells us that we will receive what we ask for. Is that true? Someone will say that they asked for such and such things and they still haven't received them. Let us suppose you get down on your knees and ask God that your neighbours house burn down, because you had an argument with him and you don't want to see him anymore. Maybe you hate someone at work, so you are asking God that your co-worker breaks a leg and someone else you don't like, so that they have an accident with their car, will God fulfil such a petition? Never, because you are not asking by God's will when the Bible say: *"But I say unto you, Love your enemies, bless them that curse you, do well to them that hate you, and pray for them which despitefully use you and persecute you."* *(Matthew 5:44)* Jesus tells us to do good to all, those whom we love and those who are our enemies.

When Jesus tells us to do good to all, and we do so, then if we ask only for good things for everybody from God, He will give them to us. But if we want good for ourselves and bad for others, that kind of prayer God will never answer and no one should expect it to be answered

In The Orthodox Study Bible on page 58 we read: "To receive whatever things you ask in prayer, one must have faith and discernment to ask for what is in accordance with God's will. God cannot be manipulated by our prayers." Truer words cannot be said. How can a person live with hatred in his heart and ask for good things for himself? Did Jesus not give us the Golden Rule saying: *"And as ye would that men should do to you, do ye also to them likewise." (Luke 6:31)* If you want good, do also good to others, to all, and you will be children of God. *"But love ye your enemies, and do good, and lend, hoping for nothing again; and your reward shall be great, and ye shall be the children of the Highest." (Luke 6:35)*

"And He gave some, Apostles; and some, prophets: and some, evangelists; and some, pastors and teachers." (Ephesians 4:11) Apostle Paul says that God gave each one of us to be something, but all cannot be the same. If people turned to God, they would not have to suffer and people would have love among each other. Look at the Israelites a few thousand years back when they left Egypt. They wandered around in the wilderness for forty years and did nothing to provide food. Each morning as they got up, food already was awaiting them. God provided them with food for forty years. Do you think He cannot do the same today if people lived by His Commandments?

Do all Christians go to church on Sunday morning? There are many reasons and who is to blame for small church attendance is the government of the land. They have thrown God out of schools and opened up Sundays for shopping. They have allowed and permitted to have telethons, marathons and all kinds of runs for different causes on Sunday mornings. They have permitted all kinds of sports to be held many times on a Sunday morning. Having all this at their disposal, do you think people will come to church on a Sunday morning? They put their priorities in different things than in God and church. Another reason could be that when you see people carrying liquor to their homes Saturday evening, bring along 3-4 videos, invite friends to come to a party when they party till the wee hours of the morning, do you suppose those people, will be in church Sunday morning? Of course not.

Why can't all shopping be done on Saturday? Why can't the parties be held on a Friday night? Then leave the Sunday to God as the Scripture says: *"Render therefore unto Caesar the things which are Caesar's; and unto God the things that are God's"* *(Matthew 22:21)*

Let us look at another problem where the blame can be put on the government as well as the people on the whole. Shootings in the schools, business places, streets, etc. Why? Since the government threw out the Lord's prayer from the schools, the problems began to multiply, not one by one, but tripled, quadrupled and more. Schools at one time were schools. Today you walk into a school and you don't know where you are. You walk into the classroom, and the students are sitting on top of their desks. Caps on their heads turned backwards that you don't know if the student is coming or going. Trousers big and baggy as gunny sacks. Noise that you cannot hear who is saying what. Some student's feet are on top of their desks. They start their day without prayer. No respect is taught in school.

How can a country allow all this and then expect their children to be safe in school. Children are being shot in schools in the USA and in Canada and now even in Europe. Teachers are saying they are afraid for their safety. Teachers have no respect from the students, because it all has become a free society, where everything and all things go. If this type of disorder continues in this country for another 15-25 years, this country will be destroyed. The students are not taught respect and obedience and they will destroy what their parents and grandparents built.

Put the Lord's Prayer back in school. Put the strap back where punishment should be meted out as the Bible says: *"He that spares his rod hates his son; but he that loves him chastens him betimes."* *(Proverbs 13:24) "Chasten thy son while there is hope, and let not thy soul spare for his crying." (Proverbs 19:18)* You can say this in other words, "Spare the rod and spoil the child." That is exactly what has happened to this country. The strap has been spared, taken away and the children are being spoiled.

Walk down the street when a group of younger people are coming toward you. See how many will respect you and move over so you may pass them to one side. They take up the whole sidewalk as though they own it. How many times have you seen a younger person open the door for an older person? How many times have you seen a young person show respect to an older one? If the children were taught about these things at home and at school, things would be different. When a child does not hear about God in the home nor the school, how can you expect that child to come to church on a Sunday morning. Some children say they do not go to church, because they do not understand the language. Even if the language in the church was golden, or if God Himself would come and speak in the church on Sunday morning in their language, you cannot expect the youth to be there if they never hear about God in their home. Children will usually do what the parents do. If the parents go to church often and the children see that, they may find enough interest to come with the parents to church. When the parents don't come to church, the children can only say: "But my parents don't go to church, so why should I?" There was this Canaan woman whose daughter was inflicted by the devil and she came for help to Jesus. She came after Him, begging and crying that He help her, and Jesus turned around and said: *"I am not sent but unto the lost sheep of the house of Israel."* (Matthew 15:24) Jesus came to His people first. We, whoever we are, should first look after our own people as Jesus did. Yes, Jesus came to save the whole world, everybody, but He says that His Father sent Him first to go to His own people. When and if we have done everything for our own people, by all means then go and help others to, but first look after your own. First teach your own children their faith, language, history, nationality, culture, etc., and then when time permits and your children know everything, go and help others too. The day is coming when God will soon have no choice left, but to send His Son again back to earth, in glory this time, so the world would end as it did before in the deluge and to mete out to each what everyone earned and deserves. There will be no excuses before God, that we were tired, we had company, we were on holidays or that we forgot. There will be no excuses before His judgement. Today as we live, each and everyone can make up and find excuses why he or she did not go to church, did not say their prayers morning and night, did not say grace before meals, etc., etc.

My late mother used to tell me that the road to heaven and God is a two-way street. She said how and what we do for God, He will also pay or repay us in a like manner. The Bible says: *"And as ye would that men should do to you, do ye also to them likewise." (Luke 6:31)* If you want God to be good to you, first you must start being good to God. Glorify Him, Praise Him, Thank Him and remember Him every minute of your life each and every day.

Remember God loves you as your father or mother loves you, and as you love your children. When your children got on your nerves, or you on your fathers nerves, then it was a different story. As long as you were obeying your parents or your children obeying you, things were well, but the moment you or your children stepped out of line it was time for another strategy. God is the same. When you follow His rules, obey Him, things will be fine and He will bless you, but the moment you step out of line, God will do things differently.

One other thing that is still in the back of peoples mind's and dear to their hearts is the topic of abortion. Some people wish that this topic had never come up. It will come up as long as people kill innocent children. Abortion is murder. The government has allowed people to kill innocent children by passing abortion laws. Why, I don't know. We elect a few hundred people to our parliament to look after the decency of our country. Then they say they have the right to decide things for millions of people. This is wrong.

There are things that the governments can, may and should do, but then there are things that the whole country-population should decide, and two of those things are capital punishment and abortion. Why should a handful of people make such big decisions for the whole country? There are groups of people who form organizations and say they stand for this or that. Then they go and pressure the government to do so and so. It seems that the louder they yell and scream the more the government listens to them and does their will instead of the will of God.

The people that wanted and got the abortion law passed, are those that either don't know God, don't live by God's laws or invented their own laws. God gave us the commandment: *"Thou shalt not kill,"* and *"Thou shalt not commit adultery." (Exodus 20:13-14)* So someone will say, what has adultery to do with abortion? It has a lot to do, because that is where abortion came to be legalized. How and why? Let us have a look.

People get together and commit adultery. Soon after, the woman finds out that, she is pregnant because of the adultery she committed. The woman has to get an abortion to destroy the evidence that she ever had anything to do with anybody outside her marriage, out of wedlock. So the evidence, the innocent child must be put to death because of someone's pleasure and sin. Adultery is committed by breaking God's law: *"Thou shalt not commit adultery." (Exodus 20:14)* Once this commandment is broken, the offenders then break another law which God says: *"Thou shalt not kill." (Exodus 20:13)*

When someone stands up to defend the innocent children that are killed (aborted), the clique or group of people jump up and scream saying that, it's the woman's body and she can do as she pleases. But it is not right, because the infant inside her, is not her body, it is another human being, another body. The woman has no right to her body, because she did not create it and if you did not create it, it is not yours. The body as the soul belong to God. *"Know ye not that ye are the temple of God, and that the Spirit of God dwells in you." (I Corinthians 3:16)* Also Apostle Paul says: *"The wife hath not power of her own body, but the husband: and likewise also the husband hath not power of his own body, but the wife." (I Corinthians 7:4)*

Only those that do not believe in God will say that the body belongs to them and they can do what they want with it. Wrong. A Christian will not say such a thing. The Spirit of God dwells in your body. Maybe the problem with today's world is that instead of the Spirit of God dwelling in some bodies, it is the evil spirit dwelling in their bodies. If they followed God's Commandment and did not commit adultery and got pregnant, there would be no need for abortion.

Then there are others who speak up and say there is too much poverty in the world today, with too many people on earth, so why bring more children into the world to suffer. This is a very flimsy and poor excuse. If God could have looked after the Israelites for forty years feeding them each and every day, do you think that God has become so poor that He would not be able to look after His children(us) on this earth today?

God could take good care of us and of the whole world as He has done for millennia years, if we only followed His laws, for Jesus says: *"Fear ye not therefore, ye are more value than many sparrows." (Matthew 10:31)* If God can look and care for the sparrows, don't you think that He can also look after man? Sure He can, for He has been doing that since He created the world. He looked after the Israelites for forty years in the wilderness after they left Egypt, than surely He can look after us too. He would look after us even better, if we turned to Him and live the way He wants us to live by His will.

One time I read on a car bumper sticker thus: "If you can read this, then thank the doctor that did not abort you." Had your mother aborted you, would you be here now? You would not be reading this page had your mother aborted you. Is it greed again? We want to live and enjoy this world, but the child conceived inside another, doesn't have a chance to live when it is aborted. Is that what greed is all about, thinking only about oneself?

I remember one year in a Canadian Prairie city I attended with hundreds of other people a "pro life evening" in a large auditorium. The guest was a retired nurse and her adopted daughter. The story is that this nurse worked in a hospital in California and an abortion was taking place where she was helping in the operating room. She said that her adopted daughter is the one that was aborted by her biological mother. She was aborted and the body of this girl (what some call fetus), was thrown into the garbage bin in the operating room. This nurse seeing that the child (fetus) was moving, grabbed it from the garbage bin and rushed to the intensive care unit.

There this child was given oxygen and other life support systems and was looked after by this nurse. After this aborted child was well enough, this nurse adopted her and took her home. She cared for her as any mother who cares for a child. When this nurse and her adopted daughter were in Canada in 1993, they both spoke to the public, answered questions and sang sacred songs. They told of this experience as they travelled across Canada and the USA, telling people what abortion is and what it does. The only thing that was wrong with this adopted daughter, was that she had a slight limp when she walked because when she was aborted, she was short of oxygen before she was brought to the intensive care unit in the hospital. That was her only disability. It was a very moving and emotional evening for all present to hear such a tragic and happy story how it ended with another life saved. So what does abortion do, it kills innocent children.

Why did her mother abort her, no one asked her. Maybe

she had committed adultery and had to get rid of the evidence. God knows what happened. Maybe the family was getting too large and they did not want any more children, so they thought abortion was the way to go, because it was modern and other people were doing it, not looking whether God is in agreement or not. But if the family was getting too big, that was no problem because when God could look after the Israelites for forty years in the wilderness, surely He could look after us if we follow His laws.

Even these abortions that are taking place each year where thousands die innocently, is also God's will. Maybe God has a plan that He wants this to happen. Maybe God wants to test and try out how well and how much the people will obey Him and His laws. Maybe God wants by His will to see if man has learned any lessons from not obeying Him. I mentioned previously that all good and evil come from God. *"Therefore it shall come to pass, that as all good things are come upon you which the Lord your God promised you; so shall the Lord bring upon you all evil things, until He has destroyed you from off this good land which the Lord your God hath given you." (Joshua 23:15)* We read that all good and evil comes from God and that God will root out from this land all the evil doers. We also read in the Book of Psalms: *"I will early destroy all the wicked of the land; that I may cut off all wicked doers from the city of the Lord." (Psalm 101:8)* To those that are abiding by God's laws, they have no fear, but those that do evil, including killing of innocent unborn human beings, God will one day root them out of the good land and the Lord's city.

It is very puzzling to see how human beings have no conscience in destroying innocent babies which they call fetuses. Look at the animals, wild or tame. When there is a young one born, how the mother stands, defends and is ready to die herself to save her baby or babies. On the other hand, how can a human being go into an operating room and have an innocent human being torn out of her body? Where is her conscience? Where is her pity? Where is her heart? What kind of a mother would do this? But maybe if they have no God in their heart, they are cold blooded and to them everything goes. First they commit adultery to break God's law, and then they destroy a human being to get rid of the evidence.

Do they think when they do this that God can't see, or doesn't know what is happening? He can see very well everything, and one day when He has had enough and can't stand it any longer, He will make an account with each and everyone for their actions. People grew up without God, made themselves gods and do as they please. They change names of things, to show and pretend that maybe God will not see or hear and will not say anything. They think if they change something to a different name, God will not know what that thing is. At the present time God is just getting things together for the great day of judgement of the wicked world and those on it.

No one knows God's plans. We do not know what He is going to do to any of us at any given time. We don't know how long each and everyone of us has to live on this earth. By whose will is it then, that one is killed by abortion, another dies in the crib death, the third dies in a car accident at the age of six, the fourth never reaches high school and graduation, the fifth dies of cancer at the age of forty-two, the sixth dies of a heart attack at sixty-four, the seventh dies at eighty-five from Alzheimer disease and another lives till 102 and dies a natural death. By whose will is it that one will suffer 50-60 years of their life from an illness and another lives till seventy-five and never was to see a doctor? By whose will does one get lung cancer and never even held a cigarette in their hand while another smokes for 70 years, lives till 90 and dies of old age and no diseases or illnesses. By whose will is all this done? The person that gets ill at the age of 12 and lives bed ridden for another 60 years, was it their will to live such a life?

When you listen and obey your parents, they will be good

to you and will probably give you everything you may ask and wish for. If you disobey them and bring shame upon them and the family, they may not even want to know you as their son or daughter. Is it not the same with God? If we listen to Him and obey His Commandments, He will bestow us with His blessings of good health and fortune. Does the Holy Scripture not tell us this? *"If ye then, being evil , know how to give good gifts unto your children, how much more shall your Father which is in heaven give good things to them that ask Him?"(Matthew 7:7)* God will only give gifts to those who worship Him, obey Him, glorify Him, live by His Commandments and are worthy of Him. One must love God with all their heart, soul and mind (Matthew 22:37) to be worthy of Him. Jesus says thus: *"He that loves father or mother more than Me, is not worthy of Me: and he that loves son or daughter more than Me is not worthy of Me. And he that takes not his cross, and follows after Me, is not worthy of Me." (Matthew 10:37)*

Recall the story of the centurion. Jesus was coming into a little town of Capernaum when a soldier, a centurion, met Him. The centurion had a hundred men under his command. What had happened, was that a servant of the centurion was gravely ill, lying at home probably on his death bed. The centurion must have heard of Christ and had faith in Him since he approached Christ to help the sick servant. *"And saying, Lord my servant lies at home sick of the palsy, grievously tormented." (Matthew 8:6)* Jesus told the centurion that He would come to his house and heal the sick man. But what did the centurion say? *"The centurion answered and said, Lord I am not worthy that Thou should come under my roof: but speak the word only, and my servant shall be healed." (Matthew 8:8)* What faith the man had. The centurion said that he was not worthy that Christ even come under the roof of his house. He had a strong faith and was asking Christ to say only the word and he knew that his servant would be healed. How about us today? Are we worthy that Christ come into our house? Is our faith in Christ as strong and powerful as the faith of the centurion was? Jesus could see that the Centurion's faith was strong: *"When Jesus heard it, He marvelled, and said to them that followed, Verily I say unto you, I have not found so great faith, no not in Israel." (Matthew 8:10)*

Jesus cured the centurion's servant at the very moment He spoke: *"And Jesus said unto the centurion, Go thy way: And as thou hast believed, so it be done unto thee. And his servant was healed in the selfsame hour." (Matthew 8:13)* By whose will was the servant healed? It was Jesus' will, God's will. The centurion had asked Jesus to help him, but he didn't know if Jesus might even want to talk to him, not alone if He would come to his house. It was on the contrary. When the centurion said that he wasn't even worthy for Christ to come under his roof, Jesus knew at that moment that the man was worthy, because even though he was a soldier he had a strong faith. Ask yourself, if you are worthy that Christ come under the roof of your house. Is your faith strong enough to get from God what you ask for? Do you think you are worthy enough to receive from God what you want if you *have not* been praying, attending church, not abiding by His Commandments? John writing his letter says: *"And whatsoever we ask, we receive of Him, because we keep His Commandments, and do those things that are pleasing in His sight." (I John 3:22)* So what makes you think you are worthy enough that you should get what you want from God?

Do not be weak in your faith and bend in each direction like the trees when the winds blow. Stay strong in your faith. Do not be like a dog that runs around from neighbour to neighbour. A good dog stays at his masters side even if his master does not feed him or care for him properly. Endure all that God may send your way to test and try you out like it happened with Job and Abraham. Whether good or evil accept it all and thank God for all His blessings upon you. Always remember what Jesus said:

"Rejoice and be exceedingly glad: for great is your reward in heaven." *(Matthew 5:12)* Do not complain that things are going hard and rough for you. If you think you are so bad off, or that God has forgotten you, just go to a nursing home and spend a few hours there just to walk around and look. Maybe then when you leave the place, you might start to count your blessings and have a different opinion if things really are the worst for you. When you see people who have to be fed day after day, month after month and year after year, you might want to thank God for your health. When you see someone sitting in the wheelchair for the last 11 years of their life, you may want to say, Thank you God, for what you have given me your unworthy servant. When you see people in the nursing home that can't speak, hear, walk, smile, eat, you might just start to think that you are not so bad off. Would you be willing to trade places with one of those people in the nursing home who need care 24 hours a day? Probably when you think of it, you may want to get on your knees and thank God for the blessings which you have.

Isn't it true how we always like to compare ourselves to someone else who is worst off than we are? You may say: "I go to church when I can and when I find time, when I'm not tired or have no company. Look at so and so, they only come to church once or twice a year." You may be right that someone goes to church once or twice a year and you go twenty times a year. But how about comparing yourself to the devoted and true Christian that goes to church fifty-two Sundays plus all the Holy Days during the year? Don't you think this other person can compare himself to you and say that you only go to church twenty times, while he goes each and every service, never missing one prayer service.

I always like to tell people never to compare yourself to someone that is worst than you are, because then you put yourself into the poorer and lower category. Always compare yourself to someone who does more than you. And how many people do you know that are in church every Sunday, they help in the kitchen, at the church hall each and every time, yet you never hear them complain. Compare yourself to a better person that does more, prays more and than see how you stack up to them. How would God reward you compared to the person that prays more then you, or always helps and never complains? When you compare yourself to someone worst than you, you lose initiative and interest. If you compare yourself to a better person then you, you will strive to get as good or better and in that way you will find more pleasure in your life and worthwhile living, when you begin to become more active.

Everything is in God's hands. He can do with us as He pleases, desires, wishes or wills. He can stop many terrible things that are happening each and every day and He can also make terrible things happen. He is the All Mighty and All Powerful. All the armies in the world put together could not destroy Him. John the Baptist was beheaded. Could God not have stopped such a horrible act? We could ask, Where was God when such a crime was being committed against His servant? Oh, God knew all along what was happening, because by His will He could have prevented that, but He did not, because it had to be that way for a reason and by His will.

All the Apostles, except Apostle John gave their life in a martyrs death. Those whom Christ taught, walked with, ate with them, did miracles in front of them, they all perished from the hands of the unjust. One was stoned to death. Another was crucified. A third was cut in half with a saw. A fourth was beheaded, and so forth. All died a martyrs death. They were all servants of God, serving and building Christ's established church on earth. So why did they die of such horrific deaths? Why? Was God powerless to stop such crimes? Did God not know what to do to prevent those tortures on His servants? Did God not know that such horrific tortures were put on the Apostles and thousands of other Christians? Oh yes, God knew and knows what is going on every second of our lives. But God's will was that those things had to happen and they did.

As already stated previously, God does both good and evil. The good is to reward His people who obey and worship Him while the evil is upon those who disobey him. Yes, God is kind and merciful to those who also are the same to others. God Himself says: *"Wherefore their way shall be unto them as slippery ways in the darkness: they shall be driven on, and fall therein: for I will bring evil upon them, even the year of their visitations, saith the Lord." (Jeremiah 23:12)* God Himself says that He will bring evil upon them. He can do both, good and evil. God has not changed. He is still the same God that was here yesterday, He is the same God today and He will be the same God tomorrow. *"Jesus Christ the same yesterday, and to day and forever." (Hebrews 13:8)*

We have already asked this question; Does God get angry? Oh yes He certainly does, each time we step out of line and disobey Him. Look at Sodom and Gomorrah, what happened to them? Was God so happy that He destroyed the two cities? By whose will were the two cities destroyed? *"Then the Lord rained upon Sodom and Gomorrah brimstone and fire from the Lord out of the heaven." (Genesis 19:24)* The Bible says that *the Lord* rained brimstone and fire out of the heaven. The devil could not have done that, because it says that the Lord rained the fire and brimstone from heaven and the devil does not live in heaven.

The New Testament also tells us: *"But the same day that lot went out of Sodom it rained fire and brimstone from heaven, and destroyed them all." (Luke 17:29)* Again in the New Testament it says that fire and brimstone rained from heaven, the home of God, the Angels, the Saints and the righteous people. If God is merciful, then why did He destroy Sodom and Gomorrah with all the inhabitants? If God is so good why did He not let things be as they were, but no, God destroyed them as He will destroy this world too. More about God's anger can be found in the Book of Deuteronomy chapter twenty nine.

Many terrible and horrible things are yet to come upon the people of this earth. God speaks through Ezekiel saying: *"So that the fishes of the sea, and the fowls of the heavens, and the beasts of the field, and all creeping things that creep upon the earth, and all the mountains shall be thrown down, and the steep places shall fall, and every wall shall fall to the ground. And I will call for a sword against him throughout all my mountains, saith the Lord God: every man's sword shall be against his brother. And I will plead against him with pestilence and with blood; And I will rain upon him, upon his bands, and upon many people that are with him, an overflowing rain, and great hailstones, fire and brimstone." (Ezekiel 38:20-22)* Wow!

By these words one may say that God is a blood thirsty god and a god of war. God is also merciful to those who live by His laws. God warns us well in advance of the consequences that await us if we do not change and live according to His laws. If anyone is interested to know more of what God has in store for mankind for disobedience to God, read the last book in the Bible, Revelations. It tells of the things that are yet to come. It is a prophetical book as are chapters 37 to 39 in the book of Ezekiel.

A very important topic that some churches and pastors do not want to talk about is hell. Many say that there is no such thing, because it is only a fabrication or invention to frighten people. Others say they don't believe in hell, because they are living in hell now on this earth. I do not know how any Christian, but even more astonishing how any pastor can say that there is no hell. Hell has been mentioned in the Bible from the beginning and to the very last Book of Revelations. It is mentioned in the Old and New Testaments. Someone saying there is no hell, cannot be using the true Bible, for if he looked into it and read it, surely he would find that hell is very real. The word hell itself is mentioned nearly fifty times in the Bible, so how can, one say there is no such thing? Besides hell, there are other words that mean the same thing and are mentioned some two hundred times.

Maybe those people and pastors who say there is no hell are afraid to talk about it because they feel that is the place where they are headed after life on earth and they don't want anyone to know about it. Jesus Himself mentioned hell numerous times and warned people to live right so that they not fall into hell. A very plain and good story about hell was told by Jesus Himself when He told the story of Lazarus and the rich man. Jesus compares our life on earth to what we can expect in the life beyond the grave. It is true that no one has yet returned from the other world to tell us what they saw, heard and what heaven and hell look like.

Jesus very clearly and plainly tells about a very rich man. *"There was a certain rich man which was clothed in purple and fine linen and fared sumptuously every day." (Luke 16:19)* He had everything, all the pleasures he could want. Every day he most likely dressed differently. Every day he probably had different food which he could not even consume it all. He was well off. At the same time he never gave a thought that maybe there is someone else that has no food or clothing. He only thought of himself so that he would have a good time each day.

At the same time as he was having his wonderful life, beside his gate was a homeless hungry man - a beggar who was also full of sores, aches and pains. *"And there was a certain beggar named, Lazarus, which was laid at his gate, full of sores." (Luke 16:20)* We know the name of the poor beggar, for Jesus tells us that it was Lazarus, yet He never mentioned the rich man's name only said that there was a certain rich man. Jesus didn't find it even worthy enough to mention the name of such a greedy and selfish man just called him "a certain rich man."

The beggar beside the rich man's gate was hungry, but did the rich man give him any food? No. Maybe at times he even tried to chase the beggar away. Maybe he did not want other rich people to see a beggar beside his gate, because that would be an embarrassment to him. Yet Lazarus was hungry. *"And desiring to be fed with the crumbs which fell from the rich man's table: moreover the dogs came and licked his sores." (Luke 16:21)* The dogs had more pity on Lazarus than did that human being, the rich man.

Time went by and Lazarus died as did the rich man. What happened to them? *"And it came to pass, that the beggar died, and was carried by the Angels into Abraham's bosom: the rich man died also, and was buried." (Luke 16:22)* The Angels took Lazarus into Abraham's bosom which means heaven, where Abraham is with God. Maybe there was only a handful of people at the funeral of the beggar to bury his body, because what the Angels took into Abraham's bosom was not the body but the soul. No body goes to heaven in the state they are in on earth, only the soul returns back to God.

When Christ returns again to this earth to take us to heaven or to send to hell, our bodies will be changed. *"It is sown a natural body; it is raised a spiritual body. There is a natural body, and there is a spiritual body." (I Corinthians 15:44)* We know only of one person whose body it is presumed was taken to heaven, the prophet Elijah. There is some thought that Moses may have been taken to heaven and also the Virgin Mary, the Mother-of-God. Do we read in the Bible the Transfiguration of Christ? So who else was with Christ during His Transfiguration? *"And behold, there appeared unto them Moses and Elijah talking with Him." (Matthew 17:3) (Mark 9:2)*

Jesus said that the, "Rich man also died and was buried." It must have been a huge funeral for him. There must have been hundreds of people of all walks of life at his funeral to see how a rich man is buried. Jesus does not say that the rich man was taken by the Angels. There is no mention by Jesus where the soul of the rich man was taken. He only says: *"And in hell he lifted up his eyes, being in torments, and sees Abraham afar off, and Lazarus in his bosom." (Luke 16:23)*   No one thought up of the word hell, but Jesus plainly says, *"And in hell, he lifted up his eyes, being in torments."* Do we believe Jesus to be our Savior? If so then why do we not accept what He says? He plainly says that the rich man was in hell being tormented. Why then do some pastors denounce hell? If they denounce hell, then they also denounce what Christ taught. If anyone calls himself a Christian, then one ought also to believe and accept what their Master, Teacher and Savior (Jesus) taught. How can someone who is a human being, a sinner, speak against what Christ taught? Either you are with Christ or against Him. You can teach as He did or if not than you are against Him. You cannot be lukewarm, a little here and a little there. There is no place in between. You cannot serve two mammon. *"No man can serve two masters: for either he will hate the one, and love the other; or else he will hold to the one, and despise the other. Ye cannot serve God and mammon." (Matthew 6:24)(Luke 16:13)*

Hell is a place of torments where there is excruciating pain, anxiety, annoyance, anguish, suffering, misery, agitation. Once a person falls into hell, that is his everlasting life. Jesus farther on says: *"And he cried and said, Father Abraham, have mercy on me, and send Lazarus, that he may dip the tip of his finger in water, and cool my tongue: for I am tormented in this flame." (Luke 16:24)* We see here in these words which Christ spoke, that the rich man still does not turn to God, Christ or Angels, but he sees Abraham and Lazarus and he begs Abraham to help him. He doesn't ask for God to help him, that maybe God could pardon him for his sins, but he turns to Abraham and Lazarus.

When Lazarus lay at the gate of the rich man on earth, the rich man did not know Lazarus then. He had no mercy on Lazarus, now that he is being tormented he finally sees that Lazarus is there and he wants mercy-help. Lazarus had his torments on earth and now he was in heaven. Jesus says that the rich man is in hell. The rich man says that he is being tormented in a flame. We know that when we burn a finger or hand from high heat or flame, how painful it is. Consider such pain for the whole body and then living with that in eternity, for ever. By whose will was it that Lazarus was a beggar and the rich man to be rich? By whose will was it that the rich man went to hell, while Lazarus ended up in heaven? All happened by God's will.

Jesus goes on to tell us that Abraham answered the rich man by telling him that he had received good things on earth, while Lazarus received "evil things." *(Luke 16:25)* From who did the rich man and Lazarus receive the good and the evil? God gives good or evil things to people as I have already mentioned a number of times.

Another very important thing that Abraham told the rich man was: *"And besides all this, between us and you there is a great gulf fixed: so that they which would pass from hence to you cannot: neither can they pass to us, that would come from thence." (Luke 16:26)* Jesus told this story of what is happening in the other world with the two men who had died on earth. We believe that Jesus is the Son of God and what He says is always the truth. Jesus does not lie. He does not joke. He always tells the truth. By what He says, we see that there are only two places on the other side of the grave, heaven and hell. Jesus quotes Abraham's words: *"And besides all this, between us and you there is a great gulf fixed."* There is a big space. An empty space, a great gulf. A great gulf between heaven and hell.

There is no other place for the souls to go after death. Lazarus went directly to heaven, as we read: *"And it came to pass, that the beggar died, and was carried by the Angels into Abraham's bosom." (Luke 16:22)* The rich man died and found himself in hell, being tormented in pain. There is no other place for the souls to go. Some have invented a place called purgatory. Where is there such a thing in the Holy Scriptures? Looking in Nelson's Highroads

English Dictionary, we see under purgatory thus: "A state or place in which the souls of men are said to undergo a cleansing process: a state of misery." If there is such a thing as a place for undergoing cleansing, why didn't Jesus or any other Apostle or anyone else mention it anywhere in the Scriptures? Was this thing Purgatory not thought up by some ordinary sinful man?

We see that Jesus tells us what happens. Two men, rich and poor died. One is carried to Abraham's bosom, while the other is being tormented in a flame. Why did Lazarus not go to get cleansed? Do you think that Lazarus was without sin? He also was a sinner because Apostle Paul says: *"For all have sinned, and come short of the glory of God." (Romans 3:23)* Because Lazarus also had sins, he too should have been in purgatory getting cleansed, but he wasn't. Why not? Because there is no other place, no such thing as Purgatory. There is only heaven and hell. Jesus tells that Himself in the story about the rich man and Lazarus. We also see that there is a great gulf between the two, and no one can go from one place to the other. Why did the rich man no go to purgatory and get cleansed. Because there is no such place and thing. Who is right, Jesus or those who thought up of such a thing as purgatory?

The gulf is "fixed." It does not move. It is there for evermore. So how come that some people believe in another place, in something that there is no such thing. People who are afraid of falling into hell, invent something to make it look like they will go into purgatory, stay there for a while, go through a cleansing process and then go to heaven. There is a great gulf and one cannot go from one place to the other the Bible tells us. If there is a purgatory, then why didn't Jesus tell us so, but He says what Abraham told the rich man.

Jesus Christ, the Son of the Living God, went through torment on earth. He was born in a stable instead of a house, lived, was crucified, rose from the dead and nowhere does He tells us there is a cleansing place. If there is a cleansing place, can we say that Jesus was not telling the truth, when He Himself said that: *"I am the way, the truth, and the life." (John 14:6)*.

If there is a place for cleansing, then someone is not telling the truth. Either Jesus is not telling the truth, or those who invented purgatory - a cleansing place - are not telling the truth. Who is one to believe, Christ or inventors of unknown things? When the rich man now sees that he has no hope or way to get out of the torments, only then he thinks of someone else. Who is that someone else? His brothers of course. He remembers that he still has five brothers on earth that are probably living the same way he did, so he begs Abraham to send Lazarus down to earth to tell his brothers that they change their way of life, so in the future they too may not face hell as he is now.*"I pray thee therefore, father, that thou would send him to my father's house: For I have five brethren: that he may testify unto them, lest they also come into this place of torment." (Luke 16:27-28)* The rich man finally realizes what is happening for his eternity, so now he wants to help someone else, and who could that be, but his own kin. Himself being in the flame in torments, he doesn't want his brothers to come to the same place and get what he is going through. He begs that Abraham send Lazarus to his brothers "to testify," to them about his suffering, about heaven and hell.

Abraham replies to the rich man: *"They have Moses and the prophets: let them hear them."(Luke 16:29)* Today, we say that people on earth have Christ's faith, His church and the clergy. When Jesus told this story, His church was still not established on earth. Abraham tells the rich man in torments, that if his brothers listen and do what Moses and the prophets taught, they need not to worry about getting to the same place where he is. Moses received the Ten Commandments from God and passed them on to the people. The Commandments tell us what to do and what not to do. The prophets came and taught the people how to live so they may inherit eternal life. They taught right from wrong and this is exactly what Jesus is teaching us in this story telling us the truth that there are such things as heaven and hell.

Abraham told the rich man that his brothers have Moses and the prophets, let then listen to them. Today we have Christ, His church and the pastors, listen to them. But I pity the people for listening to those pastors that say there is no hell. About those that teach wrongfully, Jesus said: *"But whoso shall offend one of these little ones which believe in Me, it were better for him that a millstone were hanged about his neck, and that he were drowned in the depth of the sea." (Matthew 18:6) (Mark 9:42) (Luke 17:2)* Jesus says that, "whoso shall offend," means, whoso should teach wrongfully, different from Jesus, then it would be better for that person to be drowned. He says, "These little ones which believe in Me." Those that believe in what Jesus says and teaches. This also includes adults, who are the "little ones."

If someone teaches that there is no hell, or that there is such a thing as purgatory about which Jesus never spoke or even mentioned, then He says what should be done with such people who teach or offend God's children. Little ones, means the small children, grown ups, adults, the aged, in other words all of us because we are all the children of God. When was the last time that you were in church and you heard your pastor preach about hell, that there is such a thing? Why is he afraid to talk about hell, about the reality of it and what it does to dishonest people? Maybe if people hear more about hell, what is awaiting sinners, maybe more people would turn to God and this world would be a better place in which to live.

The rich man is not satisfied that his brothers have Moses and the prophets. He is convinced that if Lazarus went back to earth to testify about hell, they would change. So he tries to convince Abraham once more saying: *"Nay, father Abraham: but if one went unto them from the dead, they would repent." (Luke 16:30)* He feels that if a dead person went back to earth to "testify," that his brothers would change-repent.

How about you? If one of your very close relatives that have passed on, came back tonight, appeared before you and told you to change your way of life, would you believe them? Would you change? Would you think about it for a day or so and then go back doing and living as you had been till now? Most likely you would go back to the same life style you are living today. You have a modern home, automobiles, RV's, boats, ATVs, money in the bank, good times, so how could you forsake all that because of someone coming from the dead and telling you that there is hell in the other world. You want to believe only what you see. When you finally will fall asleep on this earth, go to the other world into hell, it will then be too late to change and repent. Right now you can't part with your earthly pleasures, you don't want anyone to talk to you about hell. Abraham knew better, because maybe someone else had asked for the same help for their kin on earth before, and probably nothing changed for the better, so he tells the rich man: *"If they hear not Moses and the prophets, neither will they be persuaded, though one rose from the dead." (Luke 16:31)*

Look at Jesus. He was raised from the dead, lived on this earth for another forty days and then ascended to heaven to sit on the right side of His Father. Jesus rose from the dead, do all people believe that? Some skeptics come up with the funniest and queerest excuses, to say that Jesus never was fully dead. They say that He was only unconscious when put in the grave and came back to life. You probably hear many other excuses and these kind of stories. Jesus and His Apostles passed down to us to the present times, how one ought to live, so as not to fall into hell.

We see from the story that the rich man, like everybody else that dies on earth takes nothing with them to the other world. All belongings are left here on earth. If you did take it with you and you went to hell, the flames about which the rich man talks, would consume all those goods anyway. Once again I say, that I pity those people that listen to their churches and pastors who teach that there is no hell.

There is a hell and it is very real. Many people would want to come back to earth from hell, if not to free themselves from the flames and torments, but to tell their family members to change their way of live. The problem is that no one returns from the dead until the second coming of Christ will come. *"Marvel not at this: for the hour is coming, in which all that are in the graves shall hear His voice, And shall come forth, they that have done well, unto the resurrection of life; and they that have done evil, unto the resurrection of damnation." (John 5:28-29)*

It is very important to know that there are only two places to go to after life on earth is through. You either go to heaven to be with God, for doing good and living a just life, or you go to hell to be with the devil and his angels and, into the flames to be tormented for eternity.

Can anyone say that the devil stays in heaven. No, because he was thrown out of heaven by Archangel Michael and the good Angels. But the devil stays in hell, in the burning flame, being scorched and burned for disobeying God and catching people into his net where they will also with the devil burn in hell.

Nowhere does Jesus ever mention about a third resting, recuperating or cleansing area where you can go to be cleansed. We see from what Jesus spoke, that there is a "great gulf" between one and the other, so that no one can cross over from one place to the other. Once you fall into one of the places, you are there for eternity. Let no one fool you and say that there is no hell. Don't listen to those that say Jesus died for you and you are saved and don't have to do anything. Don't believe that it does not matter how you live on earth, because you will go through a "cleaning process," and get rid of your sins and then the door is wide open to heaven. There never was such a thing, there is no such thing and there never will be such a thing as purgatory or cleansing place, because nowhere did Jesus mention such a thing. Yet He certainly mentioned heaven and hell many times over.

Heaven and hell are real. Hell is the place for the devil, his angels and those that lived like the devil on earth. The day is coming when this world will end and we will appear in one place or the other. Hell is real. *"And the devil that deceived them was cast into the lake of fire and brimstone, where the beast and the false prophet are, and shall be tormented day and night forever and ever." (Revelations 20:10)* By whose will?

Living in heaven or hell will not be for a day, a week or a month, but as the Scriptures say: "forever and ever," with no end to the bliss in heaven or torments in hell. *"And the sea gave up the dead that were in it; and death and hell delivered up the dead which were in them: and they were judged every man according to their works. And death and hell were cast into the lake of fire. This is the second death. And whosoever was not found written in the book of life was cast into the lake of fire." (Revelations 20:13-15)* I pray therefore that you change your life, so that you may not befall into the "lake of fire" for eternity. By *whose will* were heaven and the lake of fire created?

Today man has made himself greater then God. My late mother used to say about people who thought they knew everything. She would say:"They think they grabbed God by His feet and they can do everything they want." Why does man honour Himself more then God, Jesus, the Holy Virgin Mary or Saints? How and why? When your birthday comes along, an anniversary, graduation, promotion or whatever else, what do you do? You have a party, a good time, you are shown respect from others and they honour you.

But why is God not given the same honour or respect? How and why? Jesus Christ, the Son of the Living God, is the second person of the Holy Trinity. How much honour and respect does He have and get? Yes, people will gather on Easter, Christmas and maybe Palm Sunday in churches. What about the rest of the year? Is that all that happened to Christ?

How about the time when He was transfigured? How about when Jesus was brought to the temple forty days after His birth? How about His name day and circumcision? How about His baptism in the River Jordan? How about His Ascension to heaven? How about the cross on which He died for us? Why not honour and respect Him on those occasions also?

What about His Mother, the Holy Virgin Mary, the Mother-of-God? Should She not be given any respect and honour? Did She not give birth to Jesus who died on the cross for you? How about when She stood near the cross seeing Her Son being Crucified? How about Her birthday? How about the time the Angel appeared to Her and told Her that She would bear the Savior of the world? How about the suffering She went through on the way to Bethlehem and then giving birth to Jesus in the manger for, *"there was no room at the inn." (Luke 2:7)* What about the death of the Holy Mother-of-God?

What about all the martyrs who gave their life for Christ and His church? How many were torn alive by lions in the lions dens? How many were beheaded? How many had tar poured on them and then set ablaze, while tied to the stake? How about the other thousands that gave their lives for Christ? Should people not honour and respect Christ, His Mother and the Saints more, but only two or three times a year? Yes we know how to honour and respect ourselves, but as for God we have given Him two or three days a year and people figure that even that is too much. Jesus said the truth some two thousand years ago when He said: *"I receive not honour from men." (John 5:41)*

People honour themselves, but not God. Let God honour you, that is what is important. Jesus said: *"If I honour Myself,*

My honour is nothing: it is My Father that honours Me." (John 8:54) Did God not say that people honour Him with lips, but their heart is not honouring Him? *"Wherefore the Lord said, For asmuch as this people draw near Me with their mouth, and with their lips do honour Me, but have removed their heart far from Me." (Isaiah 29:13) (Matthew 15:8) (Mark 7:6)* What true words these are. How beautifully some people will speak and talk about God, but what do they do, how do they live? Where is their heart? People look more for glory and honour than they do for eternal life. They worry what they are going to eat and what they are going to wear. These are the things Jesus told us not to worry about. Firstly worry whether you are going to be in heaven. *"But seek ye first the kingdom of God, and His righteousness; and all these things shall be added unto you." (Matthew 6:33)* What you need on earth, God will supply you with. Do you think God does not know what you need in order to live on earth? Jesus said: *"For your heavenly Father knows that ye have need of all these things." (Matthew 6:32)* God knows that we need food and clothing, so let's not worry about those things, but worry to: "Seek ye first the kingdom of God."

We have churches where everyone can go and worship as they please each in his own way. But this church did not come about easily. Christ died on the cross, the Apostles were martyred along with thousands of other Christians. How many people were thrown into lion's dens where they were devoured? How many people were set ablaze at the stakes for Christ and His church? How many others had swords or spears run through them? Others were crucified. Others had stakes pounded into their head. Others were stoned to death and the torture against the Christians continued non stop. They were martyred and from God they received Sainthood. Should we therefore not honour and respect such people? They were our brothers and sisters in Christ. They died for what we have today - Christ's church. Should we not remember and honour them? How many churches have put aside a day or so to remember the Saints, those that died for Christ? Yet all that happened, was by God's will.

Do you think God was powerless to stop the murdering and torturing of those that followed Christ? Do you think God was on holidays and did not know what was happening to the Christians? Why then did He not stop, interrupt and prevent it? His will was that it was to happen and it did. God could have erased the evil doers from off the face off the earth with just one thought, but He did not. Why not? His will was that the church grow on the blood of the martyrs. That is why we should honour and show respect to those Christians Martyrs.

I will mention these early martyrs again after a few paragraphs, but at this time I would like to stop and spend a moment on another topic. Maybe after people read this, maybe someone will decide to take some action and change things the way they should be. I am talking about Christmas parties. What is this, this Christmas party? What kind of party? When is it celebrated? Who invented this idea of a Christmas party before Christmas? I have nothing against Christmas parties, but my concern is when they take place.

What is Christmas? It is the Nativity or in other words the birth of the Savior of the world, Jesus Christ. What is the date that He was born? Most people celebrate Christmas on December 25, while those that follow the Julian calendar celebrate it on January 7. Whatever the date, that is not what bothers or concerns me. What I want to say is why make Christmas parties before Christmas has even arrived. If Christmas is December 25, why make a party at the beginning of December, the middle of December or even as many do today, in November. No one celebrates their birthday a month or more before their birth date. No one celebrates their anniversary before the date that it falls on, but they either celebrate it on the day it is or AFTER. Christmas is nothing else but Christ's birthday. Why then celebrate His birthday a month before it comes? He is not yet born, but half or more of the world is already jumping, making parties and celebrating. What are they celebrating, when Christ's birthday has still not arrived?

If we can celebrate His birth a month before His Birth, then why not make a Christmas party in June or August? What is the difference? If we can make a Christmas party a month or weeks before Christmas, then I don't see why a Christmas party can't be held in July. This is not giving respect to Christ by celebrating His birthday a month or so in advance. Is it that some companies, organizations, clubs, churches want to get a head start of a good time that they hold such parties so early before His birth? Is it some organizations or those that do not believe in Christ, came up with the idea to destroy Christianity, so they invented a Christmas party before Christmas? I don't know and would like to know why His birthday is celebrated weeks or months before His Birth?

No one first has a wedding reception and then gets married. No one can baptize a child until it is born. No one has a funeral service for a person that is not yet dead. Why then celebrate and make Christmas parties before Christmas arrives? It seems that the world has already gone completely of course. It seems to me like it was someone that did not believe in Christianity, started the idea of having Christmas parties before Christmas.

Christmas is a time to honour, respect and celebrate the birth of Christ. The way it is now, it has become a complete commercial venture. People just look forward to having a good time, get a lot of gifts, have much pleasure, while others even plan how to make a pile of money, etc. But in all this, where is the Christ in CHRISTMAS, the one that is supposed to be celebrated with prayer, honour and respect to Him? Christmas has become so commercialized that most people don't even know what and why they are celebrating? They have the Christmas party to have fun, eat, drink and be merry. People seem to be involved today to buy gifts, exchange gifts and to receive gifts.

When Christ was born, He received gifts from the three wise men, but no one gave gifts for the wise men. Since Christmas is Christ's birthday, He is the one that should be receiving the gifts, but does He? The person that is celebrating their birthday, does not give gifts to others, but friends give gifts to the birthday person. Why then has it become that instead of people giving gifts to Christ, everyone is waiting to get a gift from someone else, or they give a gift to others but not Christ. Christ is the one that should be receiving gifts at Christmas. It's His Birth date. People receive gifts on their birthday. Instead of giving gifts for Christ, people are expecting to be showered with gifts at Christ's Birth. What would happen if people did not buy gifts for anyone, but the money they usually spend for gifts was given to the church, which in turn would give it for the homeless, needy, blind, etc. Would that not be a better way of doing things?

Does the Bible not say?: *"It is more blessed to give then to receive."* *(Acts 20:35)* How about telling all your friends next Christmas time, not to give you any gifts (because you have everything you need anyway), but to give the money to the church, so the church can give it to the earthquake, tornado, hurricane, flood, the homeless, blind victims etc. Then you would be doing as Christ said: *"Verily I say unto you, Inasmuch as ye have done it unto one of the least of these My brethren, ye have done it unto Me."* *(Matthew 25:40)* What you give to the church or to those that have less then you, then you would really be celebrating the true meaning of Christmas. Whose idea was it in the first place to destroy the meaning of Christmas by putting up Christmas parties so many days and weeks in advance of the real date?

Jesus gave Himself completely for us on the cross and being

humbly born in the stable and not in a house, *"because there was no room for them at the inn." (Luke 2:7)* His greatest gift for us and the whole world was His death on the cross for us all. So next year, God willing, when Christmas comes along, make it be a really true Christmas. Make a Christmas party, but make it after He is born, not before. We do not celebrate His Resurrection (Easter) in October. Why then celebrate His birth so far in advance? We do not celebrate Canada or Independence Day a week or month before the actual date, so why celebrate Christmas weeks before Christmas comes? We celebrate New Years Day on January 1, not December 14 on December 8 or November 18, but on the day it falls.

Therefore please celebrate Christmas when it should be celebrated on Christmas Day or after. And do you know what else is so curious about Christmas ? Walk into the store a day or two after Christ's Birth (Christmas) and what do you hear? Not one sound anywhere about a Christmas carol. But yet weeks before Christmas the malls were booming out loud and clear with carols. Christmas parties are held weeks in advance of Christ's Birth. So all this is, it tells me that Christ's Birth is not celebrated when it should be but it is all commercialism. Companies are just out to make tons of money. Another way of making Christmas real, is all the money you would spend on gifts for others, give that money to the church, so that the church could look after those that are in need of help.

A good idea would be to teach your children not to expect gifts. Teach them to give for the homeless, the needy. Today every child has so many toys, gadgets, and gifts that homes are full and barely room enough to walk through a room by not stepping or tripping over a toy. Instead tell your child of the suffering the people are going through after an earthquake, hurricane, tornado, and tell your child that you and him or she will go together to church and you will ask your pastor to send that money to those in great need, that have lost a family, lost a home, lost everything and must live in a tent, in the cold with no clothing or food.

The wise men did not exchange gifts, they gave gifts to Jesus. Let us also give gifts to Jesus as He said in Matthew 25:40. So let us start the next Christmas and put on the parties after Christ is born. Instead of giving gifts, give the money to be given to the needy. If some company wants to honour their workers with a party, why not do that in September? If it's a Christmas party, make it at Christmas or after. Do you think God likes to see all this bustling about to buy gifts for everybody, for people who have everything? Absolutely not. Rushing about, buying gifts making parties so that they may eat and drink to their delight, no way honours or respects Christ, God's Son.

Another interesting topic I would wish to bring up of interest to the Christians is about a cross, icons, incense, etc. From the earliest of times Christians reverenced things. Some of the things came to the Christians from the Old Testament. Today after some two thousand different Christian denominations in the world, the more modern believers, always seem to say that some Christians are worshipping idols and paying respect to them. Those that have icons, a cross, incense, etc., in their homes and church are not worshipping those items, only reverencing them.

Many Christian churches have a cross on top of their church and crosses inside. If you walk into some other Christian church, look around you and you don't even know what it is. Is it a church, a hall, some other centre for gathering or what? Some seeing crosses and icons on the church or inside say that people are worshipping these things. By no means is that true. The wood, cloth, metal, paint, etc., are not being worshipped, but the person whose image is on it. When you look at the photo of your family, are you worshipping the paper or the colour? No you are thinking and reminding yourself of those whose picture you are seeing. It is the same with items in the church or Christian home.

Many have thrown the cross out of their churches, because they say that is an idol. Is it really? Is that what the Apostles say? *"For Christ sent me not to baptize, but to preach the gospel: not with wisdom of words, lest the cross of Christ should be made of none effect. For the preaching of the cross is to them that perish foolishness; but unto us which are saved it is the power of God." (I Corinthians 1:17-18)* Can it not also be said that people that carry the Bible with them are also worshipping the paper and the ink that the Bible is written with and on? At the same time you walk into the home of those who say others worship idols and you look around to see what they have in their homes. Yes, you will see pictures of horses and cattle, of dogs and cats, and stuffed animals that were killed by them and all kinds of false idols.

You see walls plastered with movie stars, rock stars, sports people etc. Are these not idols also? Are they not worshipping those idols when they put them up on their walls? So it is fine to say that others are putting idols like a cross or icon in their home or church, but when they put idols of monkeys, cats, dogs, holly wood stars, etc, that is fine. Is that what hypocrisy is, that you say one thing and do another? They say not to worship icons, cross, etc., but when they put up idols in their homes or churches, is that just fine?

Did Jesus Himself not say?: *"If any man will come after Me, let him deny himself, and take his cross and follow Me." (Matthew 16:24) (Mark 8:34) (Mark 10:21) (Luke 9:23)* Take up your cross Jesus says and Apostle Paul says: "It is the power of God." If you have nothing to do with the cross, then Jesus says you are not worthy of Him. He died on that cross for you and you reject it? *"And he that takes not his cross, and follows after Me, is not worthy of Me." (Matthew 10:38) (Luke 14:27)*

Apostle Paul also says: *"But God forbid that I should glory, save in the cross of our Lord Jesus Christ, by whom the world is crucified unto me, and I unto the world." (Galatians 6:14)* Apostle Paul did not want to glory in anything, but in the cross of His Savior. What do you glory in? Money, sports, politics, rock music, work, Hollywood stars, horses, deer? With tears in his eyes, Apostle Paul took the biggest stand to defend the cross, when he wrote his letter to the Philippians saying: *"For many walk, of whom I have told you often, and now tell you even weeping, that they are the enemies of the cross of Christ." (Philippians 3:18)* Who are the enemies of Christ's cross? Is it those that threw the cross out of their homes, churches and their lives? Is it the ones that don't mention or talk about the cross? What would Apostle Paul say today if He came down to earth and saw what looks like a church, but there is no sign of Christ's cross on or in it? Weepingly he would said, *"that they are the enemies of the cross of Christ."* People that take up other things in their lives, but throwing out the cross, Paul calls them enemies of Christ's cross, the cross on which Christ gave His life for the whole world. If I have no cross, if I don't venerate it, then I also am an enemy of the cross of Christ. I too then, am not worth of Christ if I don't take my cross and follow Christ as we read in Matthew 10:38 above.

The cross has power to the believers as Apostle Paul says in I Corinthians 1:18. Everyone knows the history of Christianity. Everyone at one time or another has read and heard about the Roman Emperor Constantine the Great. For the first three centuries of Christianity the history of the church is written with the blood of the martyrs for Christ's faith. It happened that around the year 305 there was a vacancy in the Emperors seat in Rome. A number of men were striving to become an Emperor and one of those men was Constantine. In the year 312 a battle took place. Constantine gathered his army and slowly was moving toward Rome. He would be either Emperor or defeated, after the battle will be over. What happened is a miraculous story. Some call this event "sky writing." Weary from the march with the army and outnumbered by the enemy, Constantine was worried that he would lose the battle. Looking upwards to the sky the evening before the battle, Constantine was puzzled to what he saw. He saw a sign of a flaming cross in the evening sky with words written around it: "With this sign you shall conquer." Constantine was mystified and did not know the meaning of the sign in the sky. That evening in his sleep Christ appeared to him in a dream, holding a banner with a cross on it. He told Constantine that He would win the battle tomorrow if he fights with a cross on his banner. In the morning Constantine had the eagles removed off the banners and the sign of the cross placed in that spot. He went into the battle against Maxentius, greatly out numbered. When the battle was over Constantine, had become victorious and rode into Rome with the sign of the cross.

E. Stefaniuk

The following year in 313 AD he issued an "Edict of Milan" where Christians were given the same rights as all other citizens.

Here again we see that the cross was, "the power of God." Had this not happened that evening by God's will, today we wonder if we would have our church and faith as we have. But the thing is, that again we can ask, by whose will did this take place that Constantine give the Christians equal rights and they were not to be persecuted and longer. God's will and guidance told Constantine what to do. He followed God's will, the sign of the cross, and won the battle. Every Christian should always remember that by God's will, Constantine gave the Christians the freedom which we have today. Had Constantine not followed the advice of Christ in the dream, and the sign of the cross in the sky, changing the insignia on the banners, winning the battle, issuing the Edict of Milan, who knows if the Christian faith we have today would be here at all.

What comes out to the top of all this is, that it was God's will that it happen the way it did. Thousands of thousands of Christians laid their lives down for Christ's church. Do you think therefore it is not important to remember St. Constantine each year? We gather on Remembrance and Memorial days to remember those who gave their lives for our countries in World War I, World War II, Korean War, Vietnam War. Why don't we gather and give honour and respect for the man that also gave the Milan Edict, so that Christians may be free? We honour all kinds of politicians what they did, sports figures for their achievements, and other people, but how much have the Christians stopped to remember St. Constantine?

For three centuries the Christians suffered tremendous losses from the hands of the heathens and pagans. It was by God's will that this suffering had continued as it did. All the suffering and the bloodshed only strengthened the church. When one Christian was martyred, two or more came and took his place. They were

128

not afraid to die for Christ and their faith in Him. What would happen today if the same thing came where Christians would be persecuted? Would the present day Christians die as willingly for Christ as the Christians in the first three centuries did? God had permitted the persecution of the Christians until Constantine would come and put an end to the Christian persecution.

Do you think God had no power to stop the persecution of the Christians? Do you think Christ could not do anything? Do you think Christ is powerless? Was He powerless, to stop the martyrdom? God's will was that what happened had to happen, and no one could have done anything, until God had sent Constantine to do what he did, all by God's will. Whose will was it that more than 7,000,000 Ukrainians were forcefully starved in 1932-33? In the Second World War how many thousands of clergy and laity died in Ukraine from the hands of communists and Nazis who came into Ukraine and millions were destroyed. How many were sent to the gulags and into concentration camps where they were shot, starved or froze to death, thousands in the name of Christ. How many died in the holocaust in the Second World War?

God punished people before, He punishes people now and He will punish people in the future unless mankind changes his way of life and belief. Many people say that God does not punish people, because He is a kind and merciful God. How can someone say that God does not punish people when He Himself says numerous times in the Holy Scripture that He punished and will punish people. Look and read, Isaiah 13:11, 26:21, Jeremiah 21:14, 23:34, 44:13, Hosea 4:9, Amos 3:2, Zechariah 8:14, 10:3, Ezra 9:13, II Thessalonians 1:9, II Peter 2:9. This is a partial list and there are other numerous places mentioned about God's punishment on people for not obeying His laws. Should mankind change their way and turn back to God, then God's great mercy may spare the punishment that He is preparing for mankind.

I shall keep reminding you the reader, that all things done, are done by the will of God. Most likely there come times that God has no choice but to bring evil upon the people, if they don't want to obey His laws. It is God's will to bless or and punish people for their good or their evil. As mentioned already a number of times, all things are done by His will. You are travelling down the highway at 60 miles per hour. Suddenly without any warning or seeing anything, you crash into a wild animal or it runs into you. By the time you had your foot on the brake, it was much, much too late. You kill the animal and smash your vehicle that it is not drive able. The question comes up: Whose will was it that the accident happened? Oh yes investigators will check the damage and will blame either the driver or the animal or that the driver did not stop in time. No body will say that it was God's will that the accident occurred. Was it the driver's will that he wanted to have an accident? Was it the will of the animal that it wanted to run into the vehicle? Was it the will of the car to run into the animal? It was God who could have prevented the accident by His will. This could be said about any other accident. Is there anyone that wants to be involved in an accident? I believe not. Yet you cannot do anything about it, because if God wants and wills it to happen, it will happen.

By whose will were twelve university students killed in Texas in November 1999, when they were constructing and setting up logs for a huge bon fire? Was it the will of the students to die in that accident, or in the pile of logs? Was it the will of the parents of those students? Was it the will of the university that they die? Was it the will of the Texas or USA government that the students die? Oh yes, science will come up with an answer after they make an investigation. Some will put the blame on the students, some will blame the logs that were not put up properly, others will blame something else, but no one will say that it was the will of God that caused the logs to crumble and kill twelve young blossoming lives. Why didn't that happen 10 or 40 years earlier or later, but exactly at that time and moment?

For 90 years they have been making a bonfire and then suddenly it was all over. For 90 years God willed that all was well until, when mankind had walked away so far from God, that God wanted to show the world that He still can do as and when He pleases. Many times previously I have mentioned and quoted that God does good and evil. If some one wants to call this evil, it may be well so, but could it not be that God wanted to show His power and authority, so that people turn to Him and start living by His laws? What happened each year at the bonfire? Where there large parties held? Was their alcohol and drugs involved? Was God also mentioned at the bonfires, to thank Him for everything, or was it that everybody made himself a god and they didn't need God's help? What would have happened if the students would have built the bonfire, sat around and sang hymns, read the Bible and learned about God, instead of screaming, yelling jumping and shouting, not even sending a thought through their mind about God?

There is another thing that man neglects, because he has made himself a god. What about praying and thanking God for everything you have and own? Have you said your prayers this morning? Did you thank God for your family, your home, your possessions, health, job etc? Do you just get up in the morning, quickly get dressed and rush off to work, so as not to be late? Could you not find two minutes of time this morning to say a prayer? Jesus thanked His Father for everything each time. *"And He commanded the people to sit down on the ground: and He took the seven loaves, and gave thanks, and brake, and gave to His disciples to set before them; and they did set them before the people." (Mark 8:6)* Before the people began to eat, Jesus thanked His Father for the food. Did you thank God for your food this morning or this evening? As Christians, we say we follow our

Teacher, Jesus Christ. If we follow Him, then we must do as He did. He prayed before the people ate. Do you pray with your family before you eat?

Maybe you had no time to say a prayer, because you stayed up to late last night watching a movie and you got up late this morning, didn't want to be late for work, had to rush and had no time to say a prayer? How is it that people find time for everything; for work, pleasure, sports, eating, etc., but can never find time to say a prayer. Why? Every morning and evening you should say your prayer thanking God for everything you have. In the morning when you get up, thank Him for the peaceful night you had. Your night could have been a nightmare last night. Someone in your family could have gotten seriously ill, maybe some car could have ran into your house during the night, you may been attacked in your home by robbers and thieves, your house may have caught fire, a member of your close family may have died of a heart attack in another city and they woke you up in the middle of the night. If nothing happened and all were safe, does that not warrant you to say a prayer to God to thank Him for the peaceful night?

Then again before you get into bed in the evening do you say your prayers? You may say for what? You leave in the morning for work, but what if you were hit and died by a car crossing the street. What if something happened to your child in school as so many things happen nowadays. What if your house may have been robbed when no one was home. What if you may have had an accident with your car and someone in the accident died that you knew well. What if your house may have went up in flames when you were away. If you can come home safe and sound, does that also not warrant a prayer to thank God for a safe day and ask for a safe night? The Bible says: *"And to stand every morning to thank and praise the lord, and likewise at evening." (I Chronicles 23:30)*

It is a duty and obligation of every human being to be thankful for everything; food, clothing, shelter, health, weather, peace, etc. Never stop praying to God to thank Him. The Holy Bible tells us: *"Offer unto God thanksgiving: and pay thy vows unto the most High." (Psalm 50:14)* In the New Testament Apostle Paul also tells us to be thankful. *"Giving thanks always for all things unto God and the Father in the name of our Lord Jesus Christ." (Ephesians 5:20)* When was the last time you thanked God for all that you have? Was it on Thanksgiving Day? Is thanking God once a year enough? By all means, no. Do you eat only once a year? If you do, then thanking God once a year would be enough. Do you dress only once a year? Do you sleep only once a year?

Always find time to thank God for all the benefits that He has given you; your family, house, job, monetary possessions, etc. *"I thank my God, making mention of thee always in my prayers,"(Philemon 4)* says Apostle Paul in his letter to Philemon. Paul says he mentions Philemon in his prayers. Do you mention people in your prayers asking for health for sick people who need help, or the homeless that they may have a home, for those that have no job, so they may get a job, and do you also pray for deceased members of your family and friends? Do you live with God on your mind day after day, or do you only turn to God when some disaster, catastrophe or misfortune strikes you?

I have already mentioned how Apostle Paul was converted to become a Christian and then later he gave his life for Christ. When he became a Christian, he always thanked God, for making him a Christian. *"And I thank Christ Jesus our Lord, who hath enabled me, for that. He counted me faithful, putting me into the ministry." (I Timothy 1:12)* In another place he writes saying, to pray all the time. *"For this cause also thank we God without ceasing, because, when ye received the word of God which ye heard of us, ye received it not as the word of men, but as it is in truth, the word of God, which effectually works also in you that believe." (I Thessalonians 2:13)*

The more you pray and thank God, the more blessings God will send your way. Oh yes, there are many people that are maybe better off then you with material things, but so was the rich man better off then Lazarus (Luke 16:20-31), but where would you prefer to be, where the rich man was "tormented in flames", or in "Abraham's bosom" where Lazarus was? If you take the broad and wide road it will lead you to destruction as it did the rich man. If you take the narrow road and live with God, then you will inherit everlasting life. *"Enter ye in at the straight gate: for wide is the gate, and broad is the way, that leads to destruction, and many there be which go in thereat: Because straight is the gate, and narrow is the way, which leads unto life, and few there be that find it."* (Matthew 7:13-14) Pray without ceasing that you not fall into the broad and wide road. *"Pray without ceasing." (I Thessalonians 5:17)* In another of Paul's letters to Timothy, he thanks and mentions that day and night he prays for him, *"I thank God, whom I serve from my forefathers with pure conscience, that without ceasing I have remembrance of thee in my prayers night and day." (II Timothy 1:3)*

Thank, pray and obey God always keeping His Commandments. *"Therefore thou shalt love the Lord thy God, and keep His charge, and His statutes, and His judgements, and His Commandments always."(Deuteronomy 11:1)* *"There was a certain man in Caesarea called Cornelius, a certain centurion of the band called the Italian band, A devout man, and one that feared God with all his house, which gave much alms to the people, and prayed to God always." (Acts 10:1-2)* Do not think for a moment that if tomorrow you start to pray, that you will get everything you may ask in your prayer? God is not a respecter of persons as the Scriptures tell us. *"Then Peter opened his mouth, and said, Of a truth I perceive that God is no respecter of persons."(Acts 10:34) (Romans 2:11) (Ephesians 6:9) (Colossians 3:25)* Because you suddenly are in need of something and thought that you should pray for it, you may think that God may come running immediately to give you what you want while forgetting all those who have been faithful to Him all their lives. God does not respect persons as we read in the Scriptures. God sends rain and sun on the righteous and the sinners. *"That ye may be the children of your Father which is in heaven: for He makes His sun to rise on the evil and on the good, and sends rain on the just and on the unjust." (Matthew 5:45)*

What would happen if God gave rain and sun only for the good people that obey Him and none for the unjust? Would the sinners then turn back to God? What would happen if suddenly an unjust and sinful person turned to God? Jesus said: *"I say unto you, that likewise joy shall be in heaven over one sinner that* repents, more than over ninety and nine just persons, which need no repentance." (Luke 15:7, 10) Heaven will be full of joy if someone who did not know or want to know God, repented and returned to God. God always wants people to be obedient and obey His laws, for then He will help them. *"Now we know that God hears not sinners: but if any man be a worshipper of God , and does His will, Him He hears." (John 9:31)* Listen to God, obey Him and His blessing will then flow upon you. The trouble today in the world is, that people are not listening to God, but to man. Apostle Peter and others said to listen to God. *"Then Peter and the other Apostles answered and said, We ought to obey God rather than men." (Acts 5: 29)*

As you read this, you will surely think that God is some sort of a raging monger Who will go around and punish people. Not in the least is He like that, for He only brings down wrath and punishment when people do not obey Him. Otherwise He is a very kind and merciful God. God has a bigger heart then all the people on earth put together. We must not only once, but forever remember that God forgives all sins against Him, if people will repent and live by His laws. We read many, many times in the Bible about the great kindness and mercies of God. The good and mercies of God outnumber the evil that He may send upon the people to punish them. *"The Lord is merciful and gracious, slow to anger, and plenteous in mercy. He will not always chide; neither will He keep His anger for ever." (Psalm 103:8-9)* God will not keep His anger forever, but on the other hand He can also be mean to man's disobedience against Him, and then will take up His vengeance against man. By the above words we see that God also has anger.

"*D*early beloved, avenge not yourselves, but rather give place unto wrath: for it is written, Vengeance is Mine: I will repay, saith the Lord." (Romans 12:19) (Deuteronomy 32:35) (Psalm 94:1) (Hebrews 10:30) There are other numerous places in the Bible telling about God's vengeance upon His people if they do not obey Him. It will be a sorrowful day when man falls into God's hands. *"It is a fearful thing to fall into God's hands of the living God."* (Hebrews 10:31) Don't let God's anger spill on you and your family. You should change your way of life for if you don't, your family may have to suffer up to the fourth generation for your sins. (Exodus 20:5, 34: 7) (Numbers 14:18) (Deuteronomy 5:9)

Would you want to see your children or grandchildren suffer for your sins? *"God judges the righteous, and God is angry with the wicked every day."* (Psalm 7:11) Don't let your sins bring God's vengeance against innocent people. By changing your life, God will take away His anger and send His blessing upon you. Pray that you may never fall into God's hands. Pray to Him. Worship Him. Praise Him. Glorify Him. Thank Him for everything and He will in return repay you a hundredfold and with an everlasting life. (Matthew 19:29) That is His will that He would like to see from you.

Another disturbing item that some churches and pastors teach is opposite to what Christ Himself said. How many times have you heard it said before from the mouths of some pastors saying that, Jesus never used wine at the last supper, but He used "grape juice." Many churches use grape juice instead of wine in their communion. Is that right? No where in the Bible can we find "grape juice." Juice is only mentioned once in the whole Bible saying: *"I would lead thee, and bring thee into my mother's house, who would instruct me: I would cause thee to drink of the spiced wine of the juice of my pomegranate." (Solomons Song 8:2)* Even here it says that it is the "wine of the juice". No where in the Bible is anything mentioned like, grape juice. There are many places mentioning grapes, grape gatherers, grapevine but not one place mentioning of grape juice. In the Old Testament wine is mentioned over eighty times and in the New Testament we find it mentioned some fifteen times. A good question to ask would be: Is there a difference between grape juice and wine?

No one gets drunk on grape juice. Wine in the meantime was used for many occasions, at weddings, entertaining guests, meals, etc. Wine mixed herbs was given to relieve pain. When Jesus was crucified He was given such a drink. *"And they gave Him to drink wine mingled with myrrh: but He received it not." (Mark 15:23)* He was not given grape juice but wine as the Bible says. The Bible speaks in a number of places not to use wine excessively. Did Jesus not turn water into wine for people to drink at the wedding in Canaan of Galilee? When the ruler of the feast had tasted the wine, what did he say? *"Every man at the beginning doth set forth good wine and when men have well drunk, then that which is worse: but thou has kept the good wine until now." (John 2:10)* The Bible does not say that the ruler of the feast tasted "grape juice," but he tasted wine.

Do you know the story about the Good Samaritan? A man that was robbed and beaten by thieves and left at the side of the road to die. Two people went by, saw the beaten man and did nothing. A foreigner who was a Samaritan came along and helped the poor man. What did he do? *"And went up to him, and bound his wounds, pouring in oil and wine, and set him on his own beast, brought him to an inn, and took care of him."* *(Luke 10:34)* He poured wine on the man's wounds. He did not pour grape juice but wine. Who pours grape juice on wounds, and much help it would be. Wine on the other hand is a sterilizer and a disinfectant to help in the healing process.

The Bible speaks of better wine being left to the end. In other words wine comes in different tastes and quality: poor, medium, good, best etc. Does grape juice come in the same qualities? Do people drink enough of grape juice that they can get drunk on it? The ruler of the feast says that the people had "well drunk". They could probably see more then one bridesmaid at the wedding after they had "well drunk." They could not have gotten drunk from grape juice. "When men have well drunk" means when they were in a good state of intoxication.

Wine we see from the Holy Scriptures has been used from the earliest of times, from Noah using to much wine (as we read in the Book of Genesis) and to the end of the last Book of Revelations. There are a few places mentioned in the Bible not to drink wine. God does not forbid drinking wine, since Jesus Himself transformed water into wine for people to drink at the wedding. The thing that God is against is, the abuse of wine, drinking until the person gets drunk. This God hates and for that will punish the drunkards. *"Awake, ye drunkards, and weep; and howl, all ye drinkers of wine, because of the new wine; for it is cut off from your mouth." (Joel 1:5)* When the priests went to the tabernacle they were forbidden to drink wine. *"Do not drink wine nor strong drink thou, nor thy sons with thee, when ye go into the tabernacle of the congregation, lest ye die: it shall be a statute for ever throughout your generations." (Leviticus 10:9)*

We also see in the proverbs that, *"Wine is a mockery, strong drink is raging: and whosoever is deceived thereby is not wise." (Proverbs 20:1)* We see that indulgence of wine is wrong. *"Who hath woe? Who hath sorrow? Who hath contentions? Who hath babbling? Who hath wounds without cause? Who hath redness of eyes? They that tarry long at the wine; they that go to seek mixed wine. Look not thy upon the wine when it is red, when it gives his colour in the cup, when it moves itself apart. At the last it bites like a serpent, and stings like an adder. Thine eyes shall behold strange women, and thine heart shall utter perverse things. Yea, thou shalt be as he that lies down in the midst of the sea, or as he that lies upon the top of a mast. They have stricken me, shalt thou say, and I was not sick; they have beaten me, and I felt it not; when shall I awake? I will seek it again." (Proverbs 23:29-35)* People in high positions should not drink as the Bible says. *"It is not for kings, O Lemuel, it is not for kings to drink wine; nor for princes strong drink: Lest they drink and forget the law, and pervert the judgement of any of the afflicted." (Proverbs 31:4-5)* If anyone in high places should get drunk, what kind of a decision would he make if something important came up or some emergency? Apostle Paul also warns of excessive drinking of wine because when they become drunkards, they will not inherit the kingdom of God. *"Know ye not that the unrighteous shall not inherit the kingdom of God? Be not deceived: neither fornicators, nor idolaters, nor adulterers, nor effeminate, nor abusers of themselves with mankind, nor thieves, nor covetous, nor drunkards, nor revilers, nor extortioners, shall inherit the kingdom of God." (I Corinthians 6:9-10) (Galatians 5:19-21)* There are other places mentioned in the Bible that warn to stay away from too much wine. Today we can say any alcohol; wine, beer, whiskey, etc., should not be used excessively.

The Bible speaks of many places that the wine was served for different occasions, but not to get drunk. Above, Apostle Paul says not to get into the drunkard stages, and in another place he tells to be moderate in use of wine. *"And be not drunk with wine, wherein is excess; but be filled with the Spirit." (Ephesians 5:18)* He says not to drink. "wherein is excess." In other words, do not get drunk. Why would Paul say not to be drunk. Could a person get drunk on grape juice? Wine is wine and grape juice is grape juice. Maybe have a glass of wine with your meal, but don't drink till you babble things or can't stand up on your feet.

Governments around the world set up laws about drinking, saying, "If you drink, don't drive." What does this tell you? To me those words mean, drink and get drunk as much as you want, but don't drive. Is that what the Holy Scriptures say? If you must drink, drink so that you would be able to drive and no need to get drunk. But words like above, they only give people the permission to get and be drunk, because if he is drunk someone else will drive him home. But drunkards will not get into God's kingdom.

The government says that if you drink then don't drive. In other words get drunk whenever you wish but don't drive. People who made such laws were thinking about the drunk person not getting involved in a car accident, but they were not advising the person that if they keep drinking and getting drunk that there is no road to heaven in it.

When we are talking about drinking, this also brings us to the problem of homelessness. We hear on the news of hundreds and thousands of people that are homeless. The problem is not that they are homeless, but the question is, why are they homeless?

There may be an odd person here and there having a good reason of being homeless. We can ask; where are the parents of the homeless person? Where is their family? Why does not their family take them into their home to end their homelessness?

A big problem of the homelessness is that more then enough of those people ended up on homeless street is because of their drinking or drugs. Count up the money that the homeless people spent on liquor and drugs before they ended up where they are today. If they had that money that they spent so foolishly and stupidly because they wanted to do "their thing", today they would not be on homeless street. Many of the homeless panhandlers get money from people walking on the streets. Where does that money go? If they even get a measly $25.00 in a day, what do they do with that money? Do they spend it for food? No. Their priority would be to get liquor or drugs.

What does the Bible say about those that spend their money foolishly doing their "thing" drinking and getting drunk? *"For the drunkard and the glutton shall come to poverty; and the drowsiness shall cloth a man with rags." (Proverbs 23:21)* Can we say there will be more on poverty? Yes there will be. When we watch TV at times where they have interviews with the homeless and those on poverty, what do we see? Yes there are liquor bottles around them, there are drugs, there is smoking, and all this is a waste of wealth and money and their health. How much food could be bought if those on poverty left liquor, drugs or smoking? It would not take them long to get out of the homelessness or poverty they are living in.

Throw out the liquor, drugs and smoking and you will also be better off yourself and your family. There are many people who are living on pension cheque from month to month and they can still put a few dollars away each month, but they do not foolishly spend their money on liquor, drugs or smoking. What does Apostle Paul say to do with evil people which become drunkards? *"But now I have written unto you not to keep company, if any man that is called a brother be a fornicator, or covetous, or an idolater, or a railer, or a drunkard, or an extortioner: with such a one no not to eat. For what have I to do to judge them also that are without? Do not ye judge them that are within? But them that are without God judges. Therefore put away from among yourselves that wicked person."* (I Corinthians 5:11-13)

Apostle Paul says that for such like drunkards there is no room for them in heaven. *"Nor thieves, nor covetous, nor drunkards, nor revilers, nor extortionists, shall inherit the kingdom of God."* *(I Corinthians 6:10)* Anytime one gives money to the homeless drunkard, drug addict or smoker so that they may buy food for themselves, the homeless turn around and buy more booze, drugs or tobacco. Are the ones trying to help, not furthering the habit of the homeless person? When a person is helped to get up and back on their feet, but they turn the help into purchasing more drugs and liquor, what does Apostle Paul say about such? *"Therefore put away from among yourselves that wicked person."* *(I Corinthians 5:13)* Apostle Paul himself says to use wine when a person is ill, but he does not say to live on wine (alcohol) each and every day and be drunk all the time. *"Drink no longer water, but use a little wine for thy stomach's sake and thine often infirmities."* *(I Timothy 5:23)* Do not use wine in excess, but for "your stomach's sake". What would grape juice help when you are ill? Paul says to use wine and not grape juice.

In my hands I have an interesting, important and revealing piece of document called, "Letter of God." Someone may think that this is some hoax or fable and will not pay attention or take heed of what is has to say. This letter has been translated into God knows how many languages, but the two copies which I have are in the Ukrainian language. The older copy was printed at Chernivtsi in Ukraine in 1934.The other copy in better condition was printed at Winnipeg, Manitoba, but no year is mentioned.

The first copy is in a poor condition, the paper is old, worn out and hard to read. The newer copy is in good condition. Reading this letter, one can see how much truth there is in it for today's times for what this letter says. One thing is that names of the people in the Land of our Lord are not mentioned by name as to the Patriarch or king. Still reading this letter tells much about God's truth. There is also a preamble to the letter as how it came to be. The preamble is:

"Jesus Christ came down to this earth, was born of the Virgin Mary, taught, suffered and with His Blood, He bought our salvation on the cross. This letter appeared on the Mount of Olives, in Jerusalem, in front of the icon of Archangel Michael, and was hung in mid air, written with golden letters and no one was able to take this letter into their hands. The Jerusalem Patriarch copied this letter and sent it to his brother, who was a king, to be used as a defence against his enemies. Whosoever has this letter close by them, reads it often, listens to it with attention, or rewrites it, that person will be worthy to God. Every person living by God's commandments will be worth of eternal salvation. In whose home this letter is found and they live by it, there neither fire, water, lightning or any other evil thing will be able to do them any harm."

Someone may read this and say that is only a story written by someone. If that is all the faith you have, then you will be in dire trouble in the world to come. I have read, copied, and passed out this letter to people with the hope that they will be blessed by reading and living according to what this letter has to say.

LETTER OF GOD

I, the Lord, Jesus Christ, am the true Son of God; was born of the Virgin Mary, and am asking all my Orthodox Christians, whom I bought with My Blood on the cross, that you would honour and respect the Holy Sunday and do no work on Sunday, either in the garden or in the field, because I have given you six days in which to work and the seventh day which is Sunday, I left for Myself and My worthy Saints, who are constantly praying before the Altar of the most High and Holy.

I am asking you to honour My Mother, the Virgin Mary, because she is praying for you. I urge you to go to church, listen to the Holy Liturgy; upbringing your children in a godly manner and fear of God. I'm asking you not to harm or hurt widows and orphans and especially be on guard against drunkenness; think constantly about My suffering and your great sins; do not neglect My faith before non-Christians, and always keep in mind about death and God's great judgement day.

If you fulfil what this letter teaches, then I will give you abundant rainfall; the seasons of summer and fall will come in their times. The land will give its abundant fruit. Your sons and daughters will be famous from east to west and I will grant you peace and you will be as in a dream and will have no fear. I will give you health, and after death life in heaven.

If you do not fulfil what I ask you in this letter, or if you take things for granted, then a great punishment will befall you. I will punish you with justified anger, with fearful thunder, flaming lightning, black clouds, storms, and hailstones. I'll awaken and send king against king, city against city, lord against lord, village against village, neighbour against neighbour. The son will stand up against his father and father against his son, brother against brother and there will be great bloodshed amongst you. There will be no truthful and justified love *among you. I will send great fear upon you and you will run off from your homes. Fearful fiery weapons I will send upon you. The earth will not bring forth its harvest and your livestock will be diseased and die. Your people I will drown like it was in Sodom and Gomorrah. Rains will not fall upon the earth and the earth will turn as stone and will not bring forth its fruit. These are my first punishments.*

If you do not change for the better, then I will send greater punishments upon you. I will send upon you large black birds which will fly around and will peck out your eyes; frightful infectious diseases will come upon you. I will send serpents and caterpillar worms; locusts will come and destroy your earthly harvest and there will be great famines from which many people will perish as well as your livestock. A great disease will be amongst you and your bodies will slowly rot away. Who will not believe these words of Mine, he will be cursed and will not enter into My Kingdom which is prepared for you. Anyone who shall live according to God's Commandments and have as many sins as there are stars in the sky, as there is sand in the ocean, as there is grass upon the earth, as there are leaves upon the trees, their sins shall be forgiven. Recall for yourself the tax-collector and the thief on the cross how the Lord forgave them their sins and gave them life in heaven; so change your way of life.

Whosoever will have this letter with them, they will have kindness from all people; without the Holy Sacraments they will not die and at the time of death, My Mother, the Most Holy Birth-Giver, with the Angels will take the soul of the righteous and deliver it to heaven whence there will be no end for ages of ages. Amen!

* * * * * * *

After reading this letter, it is good to stop and think about a few of the things that we find in it that shows us what is happening today. Firstly the letter says that Jesus Christ is the true Son of God. We believe that if we are Christians. Christ gave instructions to the world and He asks us in the next step to honour and respect Sundays. Do we as Christians and all others do that? Are the churches filled and packed each Sunday, or do we put our priorities in other places like our lawns, golfing, beaches, hunting, working out in the field, just being lazy and staying at home, attending marathons, washing clothes, etc? He is asking mankind to honour His Mother, the Virgin Mary. How much respect and honour does She receive today from the people of this world? She was the one that gave birth to Christ in the stable, had to run away in the middle of the night to Egypt, stood under the cross to see Her Son crucified. Does such a person not deserve honour and respect?

Farther Christ urges people to go to church and listen to the services, and to bring children up in a Christian and godly way. How can children be brought up in a godly way, when the parents don't even know where there children are and what they are doing at certain times of the day or night? He asks that widows and orphans are not hurt or harmed. How many times do we hear of home invasions where a widow is living and she is either assaulted and at times even killed. Then another important thing is mentioned about which I have mentioned previously, and that is to guard yourself from drunkenness. How many people do we see each day that are drunk? How many pubs and places where liquor is sold are ordered to close down to curb the drinking because of drunkenness of the people who bring problems of fighting, stabbing, murdering, etc.

We are reminded to constantly think about our great sins. Someone may say: I haven't stolen anything nor killed anyone so I don't have any sins. How wrong. We have mentioned that we are asked not to do any work on Sunday. Previously we quoted from the Scriptures that if anyone does any work on a Sabbath (Holy day) that the penalty for that is death. (Exodus 35:2) Is that not a great sin? This is not what I established or instituted. It is God's law, so no one can say they have no great sin. Just by doing work on the Sabbath in the eyes of God it is a great, GREAT sin.

We are also reminded not to neglect our faith before non-Christians. You are in a restaurant, sitting down to a meal. The place is nearly full with all kinds of people. There are some that may be Christians and many that may not be. There are some men sitting and eating with their cap or hat on their head and having no respect for the food they are consuming. But when you sit down to eat, do you say grace softly and thank God for the food, or because there are strangers around you, you do not want to let them know that you are a Christian or are you embarrassed to say thanks to God with other people present and around you? Why do you ignore your Christian duty to God? We are told not to neglect Christ's faith before non-Christians. We are always to keep in mind that one day whether you want to or not you will die and then there will be judgement day. Jesus always prayed before meals. I have mentioned a number of times of the quotes from the Scriptures where Jesus thanked His Father for the food.

By doing what the letter says to do, you will have blessings flow upon you. The earth will produce its fruit for you. Rain will come. Your children will be famous and you will live as if though in a dream. You will not even realize how fortunate your life is for things will go so well for you. But then there is the other side of this. If you don't listen and obey what the letter says to do, harm, misfortune, punishments and grief will befall you.

I have mentioned so many times previously about God's anger. Here the letter repeats the same thing saying that God will punish with justified anger. There will be fearful thunderstorms, flaming lightening, black clouds, storms and hailstones. And who has not seen any of these things, and lately we are seeing more and more severe weather storms. Every year we hear of severe thunder, lightening, tornadoes, hurricanes, hail, and always severe damage which runs in hundreds of millions if not billions of dollars damage. Dikes break pouring water and people are killed by severe storms all over the world. Then how about awakening king against king, village against village brother against brother.......

All we have to do is open the TV, radio or newspaper and everyday we hear about these things which were told some 2000 years ago and then again confirmed in the Letter of God. There will be great bloodshed amongst you. You don't have to go to far, Bosnia, Serbia, Kosovo, New York on September 2001, Iraq and many other palaces around the world. People have been intermarried. Wars broke out, family fight family and blood is shed. The ground is already soiled with the blood of family and friends. Parents against children and children against parents will stand and fight. We do not have to look far about these kinds of events, they are in our neighbourhoods. And even though you may show your love to others, the letter so truthfully says that there will be no truthful and justified love among people. That is so true today. How many neighbours can't get along? How many families can't get along? How many countries can't get along?

The letter farther tells us that great fear will come upon the people and they will run away from their homes. How many people left their homes in fear when the Great Ice-Storm hit Quebec? How many people ran away in fear in Bosnia, Serbia, and lately in Chechnya and other places around the world, even in Turkey with the great earthquakes. The letter says that Christ will send fiery weapons upon man. Look what kind of fiery weapons fell in Iraq, in Serbia, in Chechnya, Afghanistan, and in other places where war is raging.

Weapons around us that fifty years ago nobody would have dreamt of. Along with that the earth will not bring forth its harvest. After the Chernobyl catastrophe, how many hundreds or thousands of acres, the earth will not produce its harvest. How many droughts has the world seen in the last few decades especially in Africa, then also in Korea and other places around the world where the earth is not producing its fruit-food. And now drought hitting Canada and United States of America in crop(food) growing areas.

Then diseased livestock. Some 50 years ago or so, foot and mouth disease hit cattle in Canada and thousands of head of cattle were destroyed. In 1999 another disease of anthrax appeared in Alberta and many cattle had to be destroyed. What happened in England and Canada few years ago with "mad cow disease." Cattle are being diseased around the world, as is being told in the letter that it would happen. Foot and mouth disease was rampaging in England and thousands of cattle and sheep had to be destroyed. The earth will turn like into stone because the rains will not fall. This is true also. How many places that used to be productive, have turned into desert like places and the soil cannot be worked because there is no rain and moisture. Large cracks have appeared in drought stricken areas. But all this that we just read are only the first punishments that are coming our way if we don't change. The second punishments will be worst then the first says God.

The second punishment will find large black birds flying around and pecking out the eyes of the people. Not to long ago a movie was produced entitled "Birds." But even later then that, in November of 1999 at Chatham, Ontario, millions of crows were gathering, making noise and even causing damage to the area. This appeared on the TV national news one day. Is this the beginning of the large black birds starting to gather and they will be pecking out eyes of humans?

Frightful infectious diseases will come upon us. Do we have to look far about the HIV and aids diseases that have hit the world? Do we have to look far for other diseases like cancer or multiple sclerosis that have no cure? How about Sars. How about bird and swine flu? Serpents and caterpillar worms have already come. Snakes have reproduced more as have other serpents. Worms have been destroying trees, crops, and gardens for years.

In September of 1999 in Russia millions of locusts attacked and destroyed crops which will bring shortage of food for the people of that country.

Famines have already been upon the earth and still are prevalent today in many countries where people are dying by the thousands each day due to starvation-famine. Artificial fame was imposed on Ukraine by Russia in 1932-33 where over 7,000,000 people were starved to death. How much livestock have perished along with people because there was no food.

A great disease will be amongst us and our bodies will slowly rot away. Is this not the disease what we call today as "flesh-eating disease?" Each year more and more people are being infected by it. Can cancer not be called the same disease where bodies are eaten away? A person of 185 pounds gets cancer and will shrivel down to 100 pounds or less and then die. Is that not a disease that slowly rots and eats the body away? How about other diseases around us: Legionaries disease, Sars, Bird flu, Swine flu, etc. Let me tell you that God is always is one step ahead of man. Man finds a cure for one disease and next day another disease springs up. This has been happening for the past few decades and probably for centuries if we look at measles, whopping cough, scarlet fever, mumps, diphtheria, Tuberculosis and other diseases from years back. Man found a cure for one and then another sprang up. Man found a cure for that one when another sprang up. And it has been going on like this for centuries. Man has to change his way of life and turn more to God for His help.

All these things have been predicted in the Letter of God, and today they are all turning out to be true. Man has turned away from God and has made god himself. He feels that he now has got God by His feet and man can do as he pleases, but God says, it will not be so. It will be as God wills and as the letter says of the things that have happened are happening and will happen unless man changes his way and listens to God's laws.

For those that repent and have as many sins as stars in the sky, sand in the ocean, grass on the earth or leaves on the trees God will forgive them their sins, but by one way only, people have to repent, change their way of living and follow God's laws. By living God's way you will be rewarded with life eternal in heaven, but you must change today, for tomorrow may be to late. You must start changing now.

Many times I have already mentioned, that everything that is done is done by God's will. It is His will that we also obey Him and do as He asks. If we don't follow His Commandments, we have no one else to blame but ourselves for our misfortunes. God warns us in the Holy Bible and even in His letter above, to live His way and we will live "as if in a dream", but if we insist of being ourselves, and using our will and trying to make it bigger than God's, then disaster awaits us at each and every way we turn.

We herd on TV in 1999 that there are well over one million children living in poverty in Canada. Sometimes we wonder why there is poverty in a country like Canada. Even the Holy Bible speaks about poverty. *"Poverty and shame shall be to him that refuses instruction, but he that regards reproof shall be honoured."* *(Proverbs 13:18)* Because someone does not want to spend money on food and living expenses, but spends it on bingo, smoking, drugs, alcohol, then for sure he will be living in poverty. If we do not want to listen to instructions God gave us, how and what to do, then surely we will be in poverty and shame. Forget all the things that have no meaning in life and turn to God. Turn to good common, decent sense and instructions of Lord, how and what, and poverty in your house will be eliminated. I also was poor at one time when I was a child. My parents did not smoke or drink, but there was poverty in the whole country because of depression.

When I began school, I had to walk three miles each way morning and night. There was no school bus to pick me up at the door. Many times my lunch to school was the fat (lard) melted from bacon. That was smeared on the bread by my late mother, a bit of salt and pepper and I was gone to school. At other times when there was no fat, the bread was soaked with water, some sugar put on it and I was off to school. There were four of us children in the family and we lived in a four room house. I know what poverty is. Other children came to school with different clothes each day and different food for lunch but I had the same everyday. I know what poverty was. Yet, my parents never smoked, drank, played bingo, used drugs, etc. They tried to save every nickel and dime.

If we children got a nickel every two weeks or once a month, we were very fortunate. Besides that, our school textbooks had to be bought. There were no free books like we have today in many places. So no one can tell me about poverty. In 1960 when I got married, I got a job at sixty cents an hour. We had to scrape and hold on to every penny. Go to the homes of those today that are in poverty. Look around and see how many toys are in that house. Look and see how many liquor bottles are around the room in the home that is in poverty. Smell the air in the house and tobacco smoke stirs in your nostrils and the throat and eyes are irritated.

If a man or family spend their time drinking and partying all the time, that is one sign of poverty. The Bible says: *"For the drunkard and the glutton shall come to poverty: and the drowsiness shall clothe a man with rags." (Proverbs 23:21)*. Eat, drink and be merry and you are sure to be in poverty. If you go out each night and party out till the wee hours, then sleep and don't go to work, you should be able to smell poverty in your nostrils. If you look after your needs like food, clothing, shelter, you will have plenty of them, but if you follow and listen to the complainers, then you will be in poverty. *"He that tills his land shall have plenty of bread: but he that follows after vain persons shall have poverty enough." (Proverbs 28:19)* But even all these things about poverty are happening is because of God's will, for I have mentioned that God does good and bad to people. According to the Scriptures, people themselves make poverty. Oh yes, another way of looking at poverty is that it is all God's will. How come some people are well off to do, while others are not and they come from the same family, same parents. One child is well off and the other is living in poverty. Why? They all had the same parents. They all grew up the same way. They were all taught in the same school. They all ate the same food. They all went to the same church (maybe). Why can't all the children be just as rich or just as poor? Who controls the riches and poverty? Who makes one man wise and the other not?

We also must remember that there is someone greater then the provincial or federal government that can help everybody. Remember God and turn to Him. He looked after the Israelites for forty years in the wilderness by His will. Do you think God has no more energy or strength left to look after us today? Do you think God is now on pension and He can't look after us? Do you think God went broke and has no more money to feed the world?

The Israelites lived as He instructed them and they had food (manna) for forty years without working. Can God not feed the world today if people turned to Him? The Israelites were not all equal either in the wilderness. There were richer and poorer people then, as there are today. As so many times has been mentioned already, it is God's will that some people are rich while others are poor. The Scriptures say: *"The Lord kills, and makes alive: He brings down to the grave, and brings up. The Lord makes poor, and makes rich: He brings low and lifts up."* (I Samuel 6-7) The Lord does as He wishes. He makes rich and He makes poor. It is His will. *"The rich and poor meet together: the Lord is the maker of them all."* (Proverbs 22:2)

The Lord created all the people and He is the One that makes some rich and some poor. Remember the rich man and Lazarus. Do you think Lazarus would not have wanted to be rich also? God used him for a purpose to illustrate us a story of an eternal life where one went to heaven and the other to hades (hell).

My father told me about his early life many times. He said that when he immigrated to Canada, he got a job at a farmer's place in Saskatchewan. He worked there for a year and then saw there was no future, so he said that he would leave. The owner didn't want him to go, but said that he will pay him for his work for the year. After he figured things out, he gave my dad $12.00. That was his wages which he received for one years work. One dollar a month after deducting his board and room, and now go and live with a dollar a month. You say, that things were cheap then compared to today. Well lets look at it from another angle. Suppose things went up 100% from then to now. So can you live on a hundred dollars a month today?

I remember one man telling me that he worked twelve hours a day at fifteen cents an hour for the Canadian National Railways. He saved his money. He and his wife did not spend it foolishly, not one penny. Later before they died they bought chimes bells for one church which cost over $5,000 dollars. What my dad received in one year as pay, today many people receive more than that in one hours work. And what kind of hours? They work eight hours, time off for lunch and coffee breaks. My father did not know of such a thing as coffee break and he worked from sunrise to sunset for a dollar a month.

In the 1930's there were no chemicals to spray for weeds on the farms. Farmers had to go and pull the weeds out of the ground by hand. I remember how my brother and I when we were 6-4 years old, were asked by one farmer to pull out weeds on the farm and he would pay us. We both sweated all day and pulled weeds. In the evening we got paid five cents and a sucker on a stick for each one of us. That was for our days work and, yet to me even today those were the "good old days." There was love, there was obedience, there was justice, there was time for play and time for work. There was time for fellowship and friendship. Where can we find all these things in today's world? Today people know only one thing - pleasure, good time and money.

Even though times were tough and hard in those days, we still call them, "The good old days." People got together. They were poor but they were happy. People did not complain and make demonstrations. Today people are well off, but they are sad and depressed. In the good old days the churches were jam packed every Sunday. Today many churches contain enough people on Sunday that you can count them on the fingers of your hands. Why? In the "good old days", people were friendly, neighbourly, not like today, where it is dog eat dog world. If someone has something, I have to have the same or better. Why? People helped each other out in all circumstances. Today when something happens, no one wants to get involved. Why? Is that what the Bible teaches us? Is that what God said to do?

Read the story of the Good Samaritan which Jesus told 2000 years ago. Is it being fulfilled today? (Luke 10:25-37) People turn for help to doctors, scientists, drugs, liquor and can't find the help they need. Why? Turn to God for help. He is the only one that can help you. He is the only one that can help this world. He is the only one that can get this world out of its dilemma and back unto the right road, but people must turn to Him, accept Him, obey Him, worship Him, respect Him.

Watching the CBC News on TV in December 1999, we hear that some 50,000 people are dead in Venezuela from mud slides where villages and towns have buried people alive and where it is said that the towns will not be rebuilt, but the places will be left are cemeteries. The first thing that came to my mind was: by whose will did that many people die in a flash of the moment? Who made those people die, by whose will? Did they die by their will? Did it happen by the will of the government? Did that catastrophe take place by your will? Was it the will of the other inhabitants of Venezuela that their family members perished? Was it the will of the Canadian or American government that so many people die?

Such misfortunes happened, are happening and most likely will continue to happen because of God's will. Until the people, rich or poor, young or old, white or black turn back to God and live by His Commandments these kinds of catastrophes will continue to happen. As I have previously mentioned, that maybe it's the devils work of what is happening, that lives are lost, but God permits it to happen. What about righteous Job? Did the devil not put Job out into the nuisance grounds to live, yet God did not permit the devil to take Job's soul. The soul belongs to God and only He can take the soul away. When the first man was created out of dust, who gave him the soul - life? *"And the Lord God formed man of the dust of the ground, and breathed into his nostrils the breath of life; and man became a living soul."* (Genesis 2:7) God breathed His life into man and thus the soul of man belongs to God. He is the one that says when the soul shall depart from man and return back to God for judgement.

When we look at what happened in Turkey in 1999 with the large earthquake, the tragedy in Venezuela and other countries in the world where thousands of people perished, ask yourself;

by whose will did they die in the earthquake, monsoon, mud slide, hurricane, etc.? What wrong had the small innocent child or infant done that they must die at the age of one, two or three? Those children were innocent. They had not yet committed any sin, so why should they die? When we become older we commit sin and Apostle Paul says: *"For the wages of sin is death; but the gift of God is eternal life through Jesus Christ our Lord." (Romans 6:23)* Wages of sin is death, but small innocent children have not committed sin, so why should they die? The devil had no influence on them, because they did not know the difference between right and wrong, so they are sinless, but yet how many hundreds and thousands died. God will send punishment after punishment upon people from time to time and place to place until people repent and change their way of life. God looks with a sorrowful heart when He must cause such disasters, but He only hopes and wishes that man will see what is happening and will repent and change.

Another subject we can talk about for a while, which is controversial in nature is the topic of dreams. There are people that take dreams seriously and others just laugh them off, while still others along with churches are strictly opposed in beliefs and interpretations of dreams. How do you look at dreams? Do you believe in dreams? When we look into the Holy Scriptures, we see numerous places where dreams are mentioned, and where many famous and familiar people had dreams. Do you just laugh off a dream, say that they are stupid, ignore them and say it is nonsense or are you serious about dreams? Let us glance at a few dreams we find in the Holy Scriptures and all caused by the will of God.

At one time people believed that dreams were a communication of God to man. God foretold people in dreams what was to take place. A very good example of such dreams is just at the close of the Old Testament and the beginning of the New Testament. The Virgin Mary had left the temple and had gone to live with her relative, Joseph who was a man old in his years. It had come to his knowledge that his relative the Virgin Mary was with child. He was thinking of what to do, so that people would not think that he had been involved in a sin of fornication. He was thinking of sending Mary away to some other place farther away from himself. Then we read; *"But while he thought on these things, behold, the Angel of the Lord appeared unto him in a dream, saying, Joseph, thou son of David, fear not to take unto thee Mary thy wife: for that which is conceived in Her is of the Holy Ghost."* (Matthew 1:20)

The Angel came to Joseph in a dream. Suppose Joseph would have ignored that dream, what would the circumstances have been? Would the result be the same as we know it from the Holy Scriptures about Christ's Birth and His life? The Angel comes in a dream and tells Joseph what to do. He obeys. He takes the dream seriously.

Another time we see dreams for people to do with Christ after He was born. The Three Wise Men followed the star and came to Bethlehem looking where Christ - the king was born. They stopped in to see Herod and he asked them, that when they find the new King, they inform him, so that Herod could go and pay homage to the Child. The Wise Men found Jesus alright, but what happened after that? *"And being warned of God in a dream that they should not return to Herod, they departed into their own country another way."* (Matthew 2:12)

In a dream from God, they were warned not to go to Herod. What would have happened had they not taken that dream seriously? No doubt that Herod would have sent his army immediately to kill Jesus. Did he kill Jesus? No. Why not? Again the dream plays an important part. After the Wise Men left, Joseph has another dream. *"And when they were departed, behold, the Angel of the Lord appears to Joseph in a dream, saying, Arise and take the young Child and His Mother, and flee into Egypt."*

(Matthew 2:13) An aged man with his young relative (niece)Mary, and a new Babe Jesus, had to flee for his and their lives. Time passed. Herod saw that he had been made fun off, took revenge upon 14,000 young children who died for the sake of Christ. As I have previously mentioned, they were the first martyrs for Christ, even though they were small infants and knew nothing about faith, they still died for Christ. Churches recognize St. Stephan as the first martyr, but the 14,000 infants died a few decades before St. Stephan did.

Years later when king Herod had died, what happens? That's right, another dream. *"But when Herod was dead, behold an Angel of the Lord appears in a dream to Joseph in Egypt, saying, Arise, and take the young Child and His Mother, and go into the land of Israel: for they are dead which sought the young Child's life."* *(Matthew 2:19-20)* Each time the Angel of the Lord told Joseph in a dream what he must do. Suppose he would have laughed and shrugged of the dream, what would or could have happened? So we see that dreams to Joseph were messages from God brought by an Angel, of what he was asked to do. Was that not God's will, that Joseph had the dreams giving him instructions of what was expected of him? About Jesus and His Birth we see that four times dreams are involved about Christ, once to the Wise Men and three times to Joseph. So if dreams are evil, why then by God's will did Joseph and the Wise Men do as they were told. Why did God send an Angel each time to appear in a dream to Joseph or the Wise Men?

Personally I cannot say that I believe or don't believe in dreams. To a certain point I do believe that dreams tell of something that is to take place, of some fore coming event, but I don't believe there is anyone who can interpret them. If God will want someone to interpret dreams, He will send an Angel to earth to do that. At the present time, sleep, dream and let the dreams be.

Today I can still vividly recall of a dream that I had at 5:00

AM one morning of July in 1974. In my dream I could see a young lady running towards me, with a bridal veil on her head, but her face was not visible, only a bright blur or smudge. I could hear yelling, Help, Help. I jumped out of bed and thought someone was in great danger outside and needed help. I looked on all sides of the house from the second story house, but could see no one. This was on July first. Seeing no one and hearing no more sound, I went back to bed.

It was that same day, but some twelve hours later, when my sister called and said that her husband's niece had died tragically in a car accident. She drowned in the car which had gone off the road into deep water. I asked my sister when it happened and she said that the doctors thought she drowned about 5:00 AM., that morning. I was shocked, because it came back to me, that was exactly at that time I had a dream of a young lady calling for help. Did I know what was going on? No, but later I found out what had happened. Later I was at the funeral of that girl who had just completed her university and was to start work in one months time. This happened in July 1974.

If dreams are signs of good or bad omen, why do they come to us? How many times has someone dreamt of someone they never talked about, never thought about those things but when they fell asleep they dreamt of such and such things. A person does not say during the day that I will think of this or such and such things, so that at night I will dream of it. No, you never even think of things that you dream of at night. So dreams have been dreamt by people and people will continue to dream. The only thing is that a person should not put their trust and belief in dreams. Put your trust and faith in God and God may just reveal to you things, either good or bad in a dream. Many people dream all the time, some people dream only sometimes and some people seldom ever dream, yet those dreams are signs of things to come, only we cannot interpret them, so leave them be as they are.

Recall the story of the Pharaoh being displeased with his baker and butler and they were thrown into prison where Joseph also had been locked up. This was Joseph who had been sold by his brothers years earlier. Joseph was now also in the same prison with others and being falsely accused. The butler and the baker had dreams during the night. When Joseph saw them the next morning, he noticed them being sad and asked what the matter was. They told Joseph that they had dreams during the night, but do not know what the dreams mean. Joseph answered them: *"Do not interpretations belong to God?" (Genesis 40:8)*

The men told Joseph their dreams and he told them what the meaning was. When he interpreted the dreams of the two men, in three days it happened as he had said. One was restored back to his work, while the other was put to death. When the butler was freed, Joseph had told him to tell the Pharaoh that he was locked up in prison for no reason. When the butler was freed, he never mentioned anything to Pharaoh, because he forgot, as the Bible says: *"Yet did not the chief butler remember Joseph, but forgot him." (Genesis 40:23)* Could a man forget about someone so soon who had told him that he would be free in three days? Seems that the butler was not a gracious and thankful person.

It wasn't till two years later that Joseph was freed when the Pharaoh had a dream and no one could interpret the meaning of it. The Pharaoh had dreamt that he saw seven fat cows come out of the river and grazed on the meadow. Then he saw another seven very lean cows come out of the river and they devoured the fat cows. He had another dream where seven great healthy ears of corn were devoured by seven thin ears of corn. The Pharaoh was troubled over the dreams. He called anyone who could come and explain the dreams to him, but there was no one that could do that.

Then the butler remember Joseph and told the Pharaoh how his own dream had been interpreted by Joseph. It was then that the Pharaoh called for Joseph. Joseph was brought to the Pharaoh and had the dreams explained. *"And Joseph said unto the Pharaoh: God hath showed Pharaoh what He is about to do." (Genesis 41:25)* Joseph at that time was thirty years old (Genesis 41:46) when he explained the dreams to the Pharaoh. The Pharaoh was told that there will be seven good years of plentiful harvest and then there will be seven years of famine. Joseph tells Pharaoh: *"This is the thing which I have spoken unto Pharaoh: What God is about to do He shows unto Pharaoh." (Genesis 41:28)* People do not have the knowledge to interpret dreams, so we should not put our time, faith and trust into dreams. God will give us an omen, good or bad. If bad pray that it may be diverted from you and if good, praise and glorify God for that.

Before Joseph was sold to Egypt by his brothers, he also had a dream when he was a young lad. Jacob, his father, had made Joseph a coat of many colours and his brothers hated him for that. Then Joseph had a dream and said that he with his brothers were binding sheaves out in the field and his brothers sheaves were bowing to his sheaf. This made his brothers even more angrier. They said that they would not bow down to him. We know the story when famine arrived in the country where Joseph's father and brothers lived, how they came to Egypt to buy corn for food and bowed before Joseph who was the Pharaoh's right hand man. This was some 15-20 years later that Joseph's dream was fulfilled when his brother's sheaves bowed to his sheaf. The brothers did not recognize Joseph, but he recognized them, but did not tell them who he was.

Some dreams are fulfilled very soon as we see in the New Testament as about Jesus' Birth, the Wise Men and Joseph with Mary. Others dreams like Joseph, his father and brothers were not fulfilled till many years later. Most likely and probably all dreams are fulfilled sooner or later, but because we do not know their interpretation we forget about them, and they slip out of our life. The word dream is mentioned many times in the Holy Scriptures. We read in many places where God came in a dream. *"But God came to Abimelech in a dream."(Genesis 20:3) "And God said unto him in a dream." (Genesis 20:6)* The Bible tells us that it is God that came and spoke in a dream. Dreams are messages from God. In the New Testament referring to the Birth of Jesus, we see that the Angel of the Lord brought messages to Joseph and the Wise Men.

I myself have experienced which I believe was a message from God Himself. This happened when I was still serving the Lord at the Altar and was living alone since my wife had passed away. To serve God at the Altar was my calling since I was about 5-6 years old. In March 1985, exactly three years to the date when my wife passed away, as I was sleeping, I did not have a dream to see anything, but only heard the sound of a man talking. The voice was so deep, but mellow that one would want to listen to it day after day without interruptions. The voice was so gentle and peaceful yet to me being alone it seemed frightful.

The voice told me to get up and look into two places in the Holy Scriptures. With trembling hands I put on the light, got out of bed and went for the Bible. I opened the Bible where the voice told me to read, and I read: *"And the Lord God said, It is not good that man should be alone; I will make him a help meet for him."* *(Genesis 2:18)* I stumbled through with my hands to find the other place to read. I read: *"Then I returned, and I saw vanity under the sun. There is one alone, and there is not a second; yea, he hath neither child nor brother: yet is there no end of all his labour; neither is his eye satisfied with riches; neither saith he, For whom do I labour, and bereave my soul of good? This is also vanity, yea, it is a sore travail. Two are better than one; because they have a good reward for their labour. For if they fall, the one will lift up his fellow; but woe to him that is alone when he falls; for he hath not another to help him up. Again, if two lie together, then they have heat: but how can one be warm alone? And if one prevail against him, two shall withstand him; and a threefold cord is not quickly broken." (Ecclesiastes 4:7-12)* What was all this about? What was this? What was the meaning and explanation of this?

I had no idea that some three or four years later this would affect me. I had in my mind that I will be at the altar till my last breath. I guess now as I see it, God had other plans that were directed to me. By why me? I only wanted to be that little parish priest in that little parish somewhere where God and His people dwell. I did not want to serve in huge cities and cathedrals. I always believed that God will accept prayers from a small faithful congregation, like He will from a large cathedral. That was my hope and future as I saw it. But God changed things.

Who spoke to me that night so softly and mellow, I don't know. Who told me to read the two passages in the Bible? Who later united me in marriage to another woman, who previously I had never heard of before? God works in wonderful ways. Today I can look at another place in the Bible and quote: *"And Joshua said unto the people, Sanctify yourselves: for tomorrow the Lord will do wonders among you." (Joshua 3:5) "Thou art the God that does wonders." (Psalm 77:14)* What a wonderful God He is. Glory be to Him for ever.

Looking in the fourth Book of Moses (Numbers) we read: *"And He said, Hear now My words: If there be a prophet among you, I the Lord will make Myself known to him in a vision, and will speak unto him in a dream." (Numbers 12:6)* God says that He will speak to a person in a dream. Did He speak to me on that one night in March in 1985? He will tell people in their sleep of things which to us is a message, strange or a warning, but only we don't know how to interpret it.

Daniel also interpreted dreams for kings as we see in the Book of Daniel chapters 2-4. In the seventh chapter we see a dream, but it could be said that it is more of a revelation from God, where

Daniel sees four beasts coming up from the sea. Then what about the dream that Jacob had. *"And he lighted upon a certain place, and tarried there all night, because the sun was set; and he took of the stones of that place, and put them for his pillows, and lay down in that place to sleep. And he dreamed, and behold a ladder set up on the earth, and the top of it reached to heaven: and behold the Angels of God ascending and descending on it, And, behold, the Lord stood above it, and said, I am the Lord God of Abraham thy father, and the God of Isaac: the land whereon thou lies, to thee will I give it, and to thy seed."(Genesis 28: 11-13)*

Then what about Jacob wrestling with a man all night long? Was it also a dream in Genesis chapter 32? There are many places in the Bible mentioning dreams. What about the Judgement of Christ at Pilates judgement seat? *"And when he was set down on the judgement seat, his wife sent unto him saying, Have than nothing to do with that just Man: for I have suffered many things this day in a dream because of Him." (Matthew 27:19)* What were the dreams telling Pilates wife? She said she had suffered many things. Her night was spent in nightmares, when probably an Angel from God was telling her something that she could not perceive its meaning. The only thing she knew, was that Jesus as she says was a "just Man." From the time before Christ was born to His last day on earth, we see people having dreams about Him; the Three Wise Men, Joseph, Pilates wife....... God even gives us a warning not to be taken by dreams or prophets who make wonders of dreams and the penalty for those is death as we read in the Bible. *"If there arise among you a prophet, or a dreamer of dreams, and gives thee a sign or a wonder, And the sign of the wonder come to pass, whereof he spake unto thee, saying, Let us go after other gods, which thou hast not known, and let us serve them; thou shalt not hearken unto the words of that prophet, or that dreamer of dreams: for the Lord your God proves you, to know whether ye love the Lord your God with all your heart and with all your soul. Ye shall walk after the Lord your God, and fear him, and keep His Commandments, and obey His voice, and ye shall serve Him and cleave unto Him. And that prophet, or that dreamer of dreams, shall be put to death; because he hath spoken to turn you away from the Lord your God." (Deuteronomy 13:1-5)*

As I have previously mentioned, we should not waste our time in trying to interpret dreams. Those signs from God will come to us in one way or another, sooner or later. When God has something to tell us, He will, and then remember what Jesus said: *"But seek ye first the kingdom of God, and his righteousness; and all these things shall be added unto you." (Matthew 6:33) (Luke 12:31)* First live in the way God wants you to live, to reach eternal life with Him in heaven and all the rest of the things you need on earth, will be given to you.

Marusia had an unusual dream on June 22nd - 2001. She was not feeling to well and fell asleep on the love seat in the house. She dreamt that the front door opened. She looked and saw me in the door, but then looked again and it was her father. Her father passed away years ago (August 1964). She told me that dream and it hit me at the moment, that probably her father has come to take her to him. Just three days later we got bad news that Marusia has cancer in her right breast. Over four months later after she had this dream, she left this world and went to be with her father and her heavenly Father for eternity. Had God sent her a vision of her father that he is going to take her away soon?

People dreamt, people are dreaming and people will continue to dream, but do not waste your time in dreams. Spend your time reading the Holy Bible, in praying, attending church, helping the needy. Leave the dreams for those that have nothing else to do. If you must spend time talking about dreams, talk to the person and try to convert him to the Holy Bible, to pray, to glorify God, so that he may repent of his sins. If you succeed, you will be great in the eyes of God as Jesus said: *"I say unto you, that likewise joy shall be in heaven over one sinner that repents, more than over ninety and nine just persons, which need no repentance." (Luke 15:7, 10)*

Today in the twenty-first century we still find people who have finished high education and gained great knowledge in things around them, but at the same time they lost sense of life. Ask them why they live here on earth and what kind of an answer do you get? Oh yea, they will say that they live to get an education, get a good job, get married, have a family, work hard, retire and enjoy life. Then if you remind them that they will die and ask them what happens, do they have an answer? No. They say that is the end. Is it really the end? Is there no life after death on earth? Did Christ say that when you die everything is finished? No. He did not. Many times He said that there is life after death. I have already mentioned about the rich man and Lazarus where both died and went to their respective places after death, to the place beyond the grave that they earned while living on earth.

Christ told His Apostles: *"In My Father's house are many mansions: if it were not so, I would have told you. I go to prepare a place for you. And if I go and prepare a place for you, I will come again, and receive you unto Myself; that where I am, there ye may be also." (John 14:2-3)* Then what about the resurrection of Lazarus, the brother of Mary and Martha. The resurrection of the widow's son in Nain. The resurrection of Jairus' daughter. Then what about Christ's own resurrection after being in the grave for three days? Then Jesus also said: *"And everyone that hath forsaken houses, or brethren, or sisters, or father, or mother, or wife, or children, or lands, for My name's sake, shall receive a hundredfold, and shall inherit everlasting life." (Matthew 19:29)* Jesus says a person will inherit "everlasting life."

If you die and if that is the end, then how could Christ talk about everlasting life. When Christ said that there is everlasting life, then there must be a life beyond the grave. It does not end with death on earth. It is death in this world, but birth into everlasting life. A very prominent quote from the Scriptures where almost everybody seems to use is: *"For God so loved the world, that He gave His only Begotten Son, that who soever believes in Him should not perish, but have everlasting life." (John 3:16)* Everlasting life with Christ in heaven if you believe in Him, or eternal life in hell where the rich man went as we read in Luke chapter sixteen. Evangelist John also wrote: *"He that believes on the Son, hath everlasting life; and he that believes not the Son shall not see life; but the wrath of God abides on him." (John 3:36)* The same Evangelist writes Christ's words: *"Verily, verily , I say unto you, He that believes on Me hath everlasting life." (John 6:47)* Apostle Paul also in a number of places speaks about everlasting life. *"For he that sows to his flesh shall of the flesh reap corruption: but he that sows to the Spirit shall of the Spirit reap life everlasting." (Galatians 6:8)* Paul also talks about everlasting life in Romans 6:22, I Timothy 1:16 and other places. So if there is no everlasting life, why is it mentioned so many times in the Holy Scriptures? So you think that all there is to life, is what you see here on earth? Well people are badly mistaken, for Christ is the Truth and spoke the truth, and when He said there is eternal, everlasting life, then there is everlasting life.

How about the time when Nicodemus came secretly to Jesus by night and Jesus told him that: *"Except a man be born again, he cannot see the Kingdom of God." (John 3:3)* What does born again mean. Towards the end of the twentieth century many caught these words and began to proclaim them, that you will not go to heaven unless you are born again. But what is being born again? Nicodemus also asked Jesus the same question: *"How can a man be born when he is old? Can he enter the second time into his mother's womb, and be born?" (John 3:4)* You see Nicodemus also thought the same way people think today. How is that possible he asked Christ. People have to learn what born again is and means according to God's will.

Today those that grabbed unto these words say that you have to change your life and that is your new birth. Is that so? What did Jesus reply to Nicodemus about being born the second time? *"Jesus answered, Verily, verily I say unto thee, Except a man be born of the water and of the Spirit, he cannot enter into the Kingdom of God." (John 3:5)* The being born of "water and Spirit" is nothing more then Baptism. Jesus was baptized by John the Baptist and gave an example to follow of being born again. Just to have lived and spent your life in the gutters on alcohol, drugs, sex and then believe in Jesus by changing your life, is not a BEING BORN AGAIN CHRISTIAN. Jesus said that being born again is of "water and Spirit." How is it then that some say that all you have to do is change your way of life and you are born again when Jesus Himself told Nicodemus that you have to be born of "water and Spirit." not Spirit alone.

Did Jesus not give us an example of being born again, when He was baptized in the River Jordan, and the Holy Spirit descended upon Him? *"And Jesus, when He was baptized, went up straightway out of the water: and, lo, the heavens were opened unto Him, and He saw the Spirit of God descending like a dove, and lighting upon Him." (Matthew 3:16)* It takes water and Spirit to make a person to be born again. Jesus was in the water and the Spirit came upon Him. Is not this the same thing that Jesus meant when He talked to Nicodemus? People invent all sorts of things in their mind and say that is right. They may read the Bible, go to church, but are they right in their belief?

Today in the twenty-first century we find educated people and many Christians, which say that God would not let people suffer, because He is a merciful God. As already mentioned a number of times, God is merciful only if man repents and turns to God fulfilling God's Commandments. When man lives by his own way and against God's laws, then God will surely send down suffering upon the people and man may yell and scream as hard and loud as he wants to say that God is merciful and should not punish people, but God will not hear man's voice, until man returns back again to God. If God is merciful, why did thousands of thousands of people die in 1999 in earthquakes, mudslide and other worldly catastrophes? Why wasn't God merciful and prevented the deaths and suffering of the people?

Apostle Peter says: *"Wherefore let them that suffer according to the will of God commit the keeping of their souls to Him in well doing, as unto a faithful Creator." (I Peter 4:19)* Peter says, "them that suffer according to the *will of God.*" *"According to the will of God."* Does this not says that God permits it by His will that people suffer? God permits the suffering according to His will. Also Apostle Paul writing his letter to Timothy says that even people who live righteously they will still suffer by God's will. *"Yea, and all that will live godly in Christ Jesus shall suffer persecutions." (II Timothy 3:12)* The righteous along with the sinners will suffer from the hands of God. Did the Apostles not live righteously and each one besides John died a martyrs death and had suffered much persecution. John himself was exiled to an island. The Apostles died from hands being laid upon them. They were in prison and some were in chains. John the Baptist lived a righteous life, yet was later imprisoned and was beheaded. How about the righteous Job? What wrong had he committed that he went through so much suffering of grief, torture and pain? How about all other righteous people who lived and died from the hands of sinners? How about 14,000 infants that died from Herod's hands? *"Let them suffer according to the will of God."*

In 1999 with two great earthquakes and mud slides, some 100,000 people perished, thousands of people were left homeless, thousands without family members and no where to turn. How much suffering is this upon those people? That suffering is not over yet. There will be more catastrophes to come, because people do not want to listen to God, but do their "own thing", pleasures, wealth, sex, drugs, sports, politics, etc. We can still remember what happened in Africa, Ethiopia, North Korea, where thousands if not hundreds of thousands of people perished from hunger, from the famine that raged through their countries. By whose will?

The world supplies food to disaster areas, but how much food is needed to feed the world? On the CTV program on December 17, 1999, we learned that there is enough food to feed the world for 49 days. That is less then two months supply of food for the whole population of this earth. If any disaster should strike any food producing area of the world, we could see the world destroying itself due to lack of food supplies. People would die by starvation as even today some nearly twenty thousand people die of starvation each day.

Everything on earth belongs to God. People fight over things, saying, "this is mine, this is ours." Is it really yours? When people die, do they have a U-Haul truck taking "their" possessions with them to the grave? No. They will leave everything here on earth and will only get a house six feet long, some six feet deep and two feet wide. They will be given a piece of property six feet by three feet by 6 feet deep. Everything else they will leave behind.

All the suits, dresses, shoes, wealth, jewelry, cars, house, TV's, motor homes, skidoes, all are left behind. What you have on this earth is not yours, because it is God's. God has loaned it for you to use while you are on earth and to share it with others on this earth. God says: *"Now therefore, if ye will obey My voice indeed, and keep My covenant, then ye shall be a peculiar treasure unto Me, above all people: for all the earth is Mine." (Exodus 19:5)* Everything is God's. What you have belongs to Him. How many times have you heard someone say: "This is our land, this is our property, these are our children." Is it really yours? It all belongs to God. God says in the Scriptures: *"For the land is Mine, for ye are strangers and sojourners with Me." (Leviticus 25:23)* Man says the land is his, and God says that the land is His. Who is one to believe? If man did not create something, then it cannot be his, it must belong to the One that created this land.

People and countries fight with each other to get more land, the land that does not belong to them. God also told Job; *"Whatsoever is under the whole heaven is Mine." (Job41:11)* It is the same with the soul that each person has. It is not their soul, it belongs to God and He can take it back by His will whenever He desires it to return to Him. God is the Master of all souls; *"Behold, all souls are Mine; as the soul of the father, so also the soul of the son is Mine: the soul that sins, it shall die." (Ezekiel 18:4)*

In the New Testament Jesus also said that everything is His Father's. *"Jesus answered them, and said, My doctrine is not Mine, but His that sent Me." (John 7:16)* But then just before Christ was to be crucified, He tells His Apostles that what is His Father's is also His. He wanted the Apostles to be sure that He is the Son of God. *"All things that the Father hath are Mine: therefore said I, that He shall take of Mine, and shall shew it unto you." (John 16:15)* What about Jesus' prayer for His Apostles? Jesus says that His Father gave Him the Apostles and while on earth He cared and looked after them and did not lose none, except Judas, but everything that He has was His Father's and His. *"For I have given unto them the words which Thou gave unto Me; and they have received them, and have known surely that I came out from Thee, and they have believed that Thou didst send Me - I pray for them: I pray not for the world, but for them which Thou hast given Me, for they are Thine." (John 17:8-9)*

As previously mentioned, everything is God's. Our souls are His souls, our land is His land, our children are His children, our wealth is His wealth. Everything is His. He even has vengeance against man. Apostle Paul begs people not to avenge against others but to forgive as the Scriptures say. *"Dearly beloved, avenge not yourselves, but rather give place unto wrath; for it is written, Vengeance is Mine: I will repay, saith the Lord." (Romans 12:19)* To escape God's wrath, vengeance and punishment do as Apostle Paul says to do: *"Therefore if thine enemy hunger, feed him; if he thirst, give him drink, for in so doing thou shalt heap coals of fire on his head. Be not overcome with evil, but overcome evil with good."* (Romans 12:20-21)

Another thing to talk about is fasting, but a complete file or book can be written on this subject. But here I just want to mention one thing about fasting.

Recall the time when the father brought his son to Jesus to have the devil chased out of his son. He had taken the boy to the Apostles, but they could not chase the devil out of the boy. The devil had been throwing the young boy into the fire and at times into the water to destroy him, to kill him. The devil tried to destroy the boy, but God's will was, that the boy would not perish. God's will was greater then the devil's.

When the young lad was brought to Jesus, Jesus rebuked the devil and the young lad was immediately made well. *"And Jesus rebuked the devil; and he departed out of him: and the child was cured from that very hour."* (Matthew 17:18) Later came a lesson to the Apostles which we today also learn. When they were alone with Jesus they asked Jesus why they couldn't chase the devil out of the boy. What Jesus told the Apostles then, He is telling us the same today? *"Howbeit this kind goes not out but by prayer and fasting."* (Matthew 17:21) You may be a person looking for peace and quiet, but can not find it. Why? You may say that the devil is causing all the problems in the world, wars, floods, earthquakes, etc. You say that you pray and still people die from aids, cancer and all other sorts of diseases and God is not hearing your prayer. Oh no, God hears your prayer very well, but you must obey God if you want Him to fulfil your prayers. But God is leaving that up to you to chase the devil away and stop him from causing all kinds of problems around you. You will probably ask - how? The answer is, by PRAYER and FASTING. Isn't that what Jesus said that you need both to chase away the devil? You pray, but you get no answer and results to your problems. You are lacking one other thing, - you also need fasting. Prayer and fasting are like a bird with two wings. With two strong wings it can fly and soar high up into the sky. If one wing is weak or broken, the bird will not fly. The same with your petition to God, it must fly on two wings, of "prayer and fasting." Chasing the devil away from yourself, you need prayer and fasting.

Did Cornelius not fast and pray. Not by prayer alone, but also with fasting.*"And Cornelius said, Four days ago I was fasting until this hour; and at the ninth hour I prayed in my house, and behold, a man stood before me in bright clothing." (Acts 10:30)* We see again in Acts of the Apostles that prayer and fasting go together even when ordination takes place. *"As they ministered to the Lord and fasted, the Holy Spirit said, "Now separate to Me Barnabas and Saul for the work to which I have called them." Then having fasted and prayed, and laid hands on them, they sent them away." (Acts 13:2-3)*

When Jesus was brought to the temple on the fortieth day after His birth, there in the temple were Simeon and a woman named Anna. What was this woman doing in the temple? We know that she had been a widow for a long time. *"And she was a widow of about four score and four years, which departed not from the temple, but served God with fasting and prayers night and day." (Luke 2:37)* She served God with two things, "fasting and prayer." How is it that many people just spend time praying, but they do not have anything to do with fasting? Many important people fasted as we read in the Holy Scriptures, so why has fasting been eliminated by some churches and others do not even recognize it?

Yes there are some Christian and non-Christian denominations that talk and say that they have advent or fast, but if they have fast, what do they do during that time? Oh yes, they have Christmas parties, where they can drink, eat, dance and enjoy themselves in full pleasure. Is that fasting? Fasting is abstinence from pleasures. Fasting is a time for prayer and meditation not good times. So is that fasting when you see thousands of people jumping, twirling, yelling, screaming during the advent or fast period. In which holy book does it says that fasting is a time for enjoyment and pleasure? What do we hear on the radio and see on the TV? Did Jesus, Moses, Elijah or anyone else dance, yell, shout and scream when they were fasting? I believe not. They were quiet, prayed and meditated. What kind of fasting is there during Advent when tables are laden with food, drink, alcohol and music pounding that the ear drums are just about at the bursting position.

When advent or fast period is on, do we see any fasting? The wild music of rock and roll pierces one's ears that the radio or TV must be turned off. Wild, insane, maddening, fanatical music is played on the radios, TV and at home on record players or CD's. During advent, Christmas parties are put on with wild music and noise for people's enjoyment and tables are laden with food. After the party, people are going home, some in a wild state, some drunkenness and some are stopped by police on the roads. Is that a fasting period called Advent? We can read in the Old Testament how King Darius fasted. King Darius had commanded that Daniel be thrown into the lions den, so that the lions may devour him. This was done and the king himself sealed the den with the hope that in the morning there would only remain a pile of bones of Daniel. That evening the king fasted. How? *"Then the king went to his palace, and passed the night fasting: neither were instruments of music brought before him: and his sleep went from him." (Daniel 6:18)*

When Jesus, Moses, Elijah or anyone else fasted, was there great music and enjoyment, yelling and screaming? One cannot pray and fast when tables are laden with food and drink, with screaming music pounding the people's eardrums. Fasting is supposed to be a time of peace, quiet, meditation and prayer. To fast is to hold back, cut down, decrease, abstain. Then there are some people who say they don't eat meat during lent. Big deal. One of the great church teachers of the early church said: "What good is it for you that you say you don't eat meat during the fast, but with your mouth you tear your neighbour apart."

Fast with your eyes by not looking at things you love to see and know that you should not look at it. With your mouth you can fast by not saying evil, bad or awful things about others. In other words, do not lie, do not gossip, do no swear. Especially cut down on foul language. Don't let your hands take things that are not yours. Your feet can help in the fasting, by walking away from evil, but by walking towards God, His Commandments and church. Don't let your feet take you where wrong is done. Walk away from the bad. With your heart you can fast by showing kindness to others. Show your mercy to those who need help. There is what we call the Golden Rule, and that comes from the Bible saying, "Do unto others as you want others to do to you." This Golden Rule was given to the world by none other than Christ when He said: *"And as ye would that man should do to you, do ye also to them likewise." (Luke 6:31)* Do good to others and others in return will repay you with the same goodness. When you do good and have mercy to others, God will be merciful to you too. During the fast period take time to pray and fast. Fasting never hurts anyone, but brings benefit to both the body and soul.

Every year at year end, companies, stores, factories, governments take stock or inventory of their work of the past year. A person during fast should also take inventory of their body and soul. At the end of the fast season, did you become a better person than you were when you started to fast? Have you prayed more often? Did you attend church more regularly? Did you stop swearing and using foul language? During fast, have you eaten less or none of the things you enjoy? Fast is a time to refrain from all worldly pleasures and a time to feed your soul. The Bible talks in many places about fasting and a great benefit will come to everyone who fasts.

In today's technological world, man has turned aside God's laws, changed them, even thrown them out and in place made his own laws or not following any laws at all. Man does as the young in the world say today, "Everything goes." Because God's laws are greater and stronger than man's laws, sooner or later He will bring down His wrath and anger upon man as has already been stated many times above.

Every year we hear during the period of Christ's Nativity that people are celebrating Ukrainian Christmas on January 7th. For many years I have been telling people that there is no such thing as Ukrainian Christmas. Is there such a thing as Irish Christmas, German Christmas, African Christmas, Brazilian Christmas, Roman Christmas etc. There are other nationalities that celebrate Christ's Nativity on January 7th, but you don't hear anyone say that it is Russian Christmas, or Serbian Christmas. So why do we say Ukrainian Christmas. People that adhere to the Julian calendar whether they be Ukrainians, Russians, Bulgarians, White Russians, Romanians and others, celebrate Christ's Nativity on January 7th. They all celebrate the Orthodox Nativity or as some call Christmas. Yes, there are some Ukrainians who are not Orthodox, but who adopted the Gregorian Calendar and celebrate Christmas on December 25th, but we don't hear anyone saying that its Ukrainian Christmas. There are Ukrainians that celebrate Christmas on December 25th, but no one says its Ukrainian Christmas. Orthodox countries and nationalities that still adhere to the Julian Calendar are the ones that celebrate Christ's Nativity on January 7th and it should be called Orthodox Christmas and not Ukrainian Christmas.

God does not only punish people for their disobedience to Him, but He also blesses those that obey Him and His laws. He is a Merciful God and will give mercy to those who honour and respect Him. To fear the Lord is to obey Him, worship Him, fulfil His Commandments. The Scriptures mention numerous times of the blessings which God sends down upon His people. *"He will bless them that fear the Lord, both small and great." (Psalm 115:13)* We also read, *"Save when there shall be no poor among you; for the Lord shall greatly bless thee in the land which the Lord thy God gives thee for an inheritance to possess it." (Deuteronomy 15:4)*

In another place we read, *"For thou Lord, wilt bless the righteous; with favour wilt thou compass him as with a shield." (Psalm 5:12)* After God created the world, and the first people Adam and Eve, He blessed them. *"And God blessed them, and God said unto them, Be fruitful, and multiply, and replenish the earth, and subdue it; and have dominion over the fish of the sea, and over the fowl of the air, and over everything that moves upon the earth." (Genesis 1:28)*

When God created the world, He blessed everything, because everything was good as the Bible tells us, *"And God called the dry land Earth; and the gathering together of the waters He called seas: and God saw that it was good." (Genesis 1:10)* We find the same in Genesis 1:12, 18, 21, 25. What happened on the seventh day after God had created everything on earth? We read in the Bible, *"And God blessed the seventh day and sanctified it." (Genesis 2:3)* God blesses everyone that obeys Him. *"And all these blessings shall come on these, and overtake thee, if thou shalt hearken unto the voice of the Lord thy God." (Deuteronomy 28:2)* There are many, many other places mentioned in the Bible that God will bless those who obey Him and live by His laws and His will. God is stronger than man and His law is greater and stronger than man's laws or regulations.

Another important thing that Jesus said when He was on earth, was that He categorized dead people into two categories. How can there be two categories of dead people? When they are dead, they are dead. In order to know more and understand this we must go to the Holy Scriptures and see for ourselves what Christ had to say. We read: *"Most assuredly, I say unto you, the hour is coming, and now is, when the dead will hear the voice of the Son of God; and those who hear will live." (John 5:25)* These words immediately strike us as to people who have died, are in the graves and will one day arise and live as we know will happen when Christ comes to the earth the second time.

But this is not so. The dead about which Christ is speaking in the above verse are not people in the graves, but what I call them as, "walking skeletons", on the face of the earth. How many people do you know who are your relatives, friends or neighbours that never come to church. They never assist or give a hand in anything. They never do any good to anyone. So when such people live in that way, can you say that they are alive to God, the church, family, etc? Can the people in the graves help us with anything? Can they come to church and help sing in the choir? Can they come and help us clean our house? Can those in the graves help in our yard work or in the garden, etc? No, they can't, for they are in the graves. They do not benefit us or the world. When someone is living in a way that they think only of themselves forgetting their family, neighbours, country, etc., then can you call such people as alive? They are the ones that Christ calls dead - of one category. They are like "walking skeletons" on the face of this earth. No one has any benefit or good from them, so Christ says they are dead in the eyes of the Lord.

Jesus said; *"I say to you, the hour is coming, and now is, when the dead will hear the voice of the Son of God; and those who hear will live." (John 5:25)* How many times in Christ's time on earth did people hear His voice and become His followers and Christians? Maybe they too were dead to the world, but they became alive hearing Christ and later gave their lives for Him. How about in our time? Are there any who hear His voice and become alive? Yes there are. How many have been alcoholics, drug addicts, in prison for some crime, but they heard Christ's words and they changed their way of life and in that way became alive. How many that were dead to society have become alive? So this is one category of dead people that were in Christ's time and we find them in our day too.

When we read a few lines farther, we find the following words: *"Do not marvel at this; for the hour is coming in which all who are in the graves will hear His voice and will come forth."* *(John 5:28)* Here Jesus plainly speaks that, "those who are in the graves", will become alive. There were people in Jesus' time who became alive who had been in the graves. The brother of Mary and Martha, Lazarus, had been in the grave for four days when he was resurrected by Christ. *"Martha, the sister of him who was dead said to Him, Lord, by this time there is stench, for he has been dead four days." (John 11:39)*

When Jesus was crucified many dead people also arose from the graves. *"And the graves were opened; and many bodies of the saints who had fallen asleep were raised." (Matthew 27:52)* As for the resurrection of all the rest of the deceased who are in the graves, the time has yet to come for we read; *"For the Lord Himself will descend from heaven with a shout, with the voice of an Archangel, and with the trumpet of God. And the dead in Christ will rise first."* *(I Thessalonians 4:16)*

So we see two categories of dead people as Christ sees them and tells us about them. Those who are dead and in the graves and the others that are dead as I call them "walking skeletons" on this earth that have not brought any good to God, His Church, our community, organization, etc. Ask yourself, to which group of dead people are you numbered? Check and see to which group your family, relatives, friends, belong - to those in the graves or as "walking skeletons?" Are they fulfilling the wishes of God and doing His will? Are they in church on Sunday? Do they say grace before meals? Do they help the needy, homeless, storm ravaged people or do they just think of themselves?

One time in a church before the services were even started, there was talk that God is punishing people with a drought. The pastor of that congregation says: "God is merciful, He never punishes." I could not agree with such a statement for one bit. How could someone say that God does not punish when God Himself said: *"The Lord is long-suffering, and of great mercy, forgiving iniquity and transgression, and by no means clearing the guilty, visiting the iniquity of the fathers upon the children unto the third and fourth generation." (Numbers 14:18)* Also the same is found in Exodus 20:5 and Deuteronomy 5:9.

"This is in the Old Testament" some will say. Well what does the New Testament say? Let us glance at the poor man that lay near the pool of Bethesda for 38 years. That's right, 38 years. He lay by the pool to get into the pool when the Angel stirs the water, and the first person to step into the water became well whatever their illness. This man could not move fast enough to get into the water and laid there for thirty-eight years. *"And a certain man was there, which had an infirmity thirty-eight years." (John 5:5)*

Jesus made the man well. Read the story in John 5:1-15. After the man was well, where did he go? The Bible tells us: *"After ward Jesus finds him in the temple......." (John 5:14)* Of course he went to the temple to thank God for being made well. Jesus also told him one other very important thing. *"Behold, thou art made whole: sin no more, lest a worse thing come unto thee." (John 5:14)* A man laying for 38 years made well, and then Jesus says that he not sin anymore so that something worst not come upon him. So thirty-eight years of being a cripple was not worst enough for that man? Yet Jesus says that something worst could come. If something worst could come, from who would it come? From you, from me, from the neighbours? Only God can make things good or bad. Jesus said: *"Sin no more, lest a worse thing come unto thee.*" So payment for sin is punishment from God. That is what Jesus says.

My mother when she was still living always used to tell many truths in a special way. Many times she said: "We make plans and God changes them." How true that is. She also used to tell me: "Eugene, God does not punish people with a whip." That also is so true. Did you ever see God punish someone with a whip for doing something wrong - sinning? No. But God will send His punishment upon His people in different ways. He will send a drought, famine, tornado, hurricane, earthquake, flood, fire, diseases, locusts, etc. He will do that until people change their way and turn to God. That is His will.

Recall another event in Apostle Paul's life. He himself turns to God to help him, to take away the thorn that was bothering him. We don't know what the thorn was. Was it a painful leg condition? Was it some boil or ulcer in his leg? Was it a birth deformity? We don't know, but we know that Apostle Paul asked God three times to remove that pain from him, but God did not. We read about Paul's suffering. *"And lest I should be exalted above measure through the abundance of the revelations, there was given to me a thorn in the flesh, the messenger of Satan to buffet me, lest I should be exalted above measure. For this thing I besought the Lord thrice, that it might depart from me. And He said unto me, 'My grace is sufficient for thee: for My strength is made perfect in weakness."* (II Corinthians 12:7-9)

Paul says that the messenger of Satan came to buffet him. God gave permission for Satan to put pain to Paul, as had happened in the Old Testament to the Righteous Job. Paul asked God three times to remove the pain, but God would not do it. God's will was that Paul had to live and carry on the best he could with his pain.

We heard of the tragic event that happened on August 24 - 2001. A jet plane with over 300 people on board ran out of fuel. The plane flew for 18 minutes without fuel and no engines running. Death was a sure thing for the passengers. When the plane had finally ended up on the ground, there were 9 people injured. No one perished. All were saved from death. By whose will did that occur? Was there a number of passengers who wanted the plane to run out of fuel and crash? Did the pilot want the plane to crash? By whose will were there no deaths? God's Angels carried the plane down to safety and no one was killed in the tragic event. By whose will?

One last item I wish to give another example of God's will. When I was serving the congregation in Dauphin, Manitoba, one parishioner stood up at a monthly church meeting and asked if the congregation had any older priest's vestments that were not being used. He had been to Phoenix Arizona and visited a newly organized congregation. The congregation was poor. Not many parishioners. No finances. The congregation passed a motion that I look and see it there are any vestments that I do not use for services. If there are that we send to the congregation in Phoenix two vestments.

A few days later I checked the vestment closet and saw a few older vestments that I was not using and no one else would use because the congregation has many new vestments. I packed two pairs of vestments and sent them away to Phoenix, Arizona. Now let us think by whose will all this transpired? Of course by God's will. God sent the parishioner to Phoenix, by the will of God the congregation made a decision, and by God's will I sent the vestments to the priest in Phoenix.

Do you know what happened later? God work's in wondrous ways by His will. Some twenty years after the vestments were sent to Phoenix, I was serving that congregation in Phoenix 1993-1996 and do you know what was happening? Yes maybe you guessed correctly. I was serving and using those vestments for services. Had some one told me on the day I mailed the vestments from

Dauphin, that I one day would wear those vestments during a service, I would have told that person, that they did not know what they were talking about.

Yes God's will was, is and will be always working out how He wants and not you or me. God works in wondrous ways by the things that happen with and to us each day. Only a mind like no other can accomplish such wondrous actions.

May God be our helper and be by our side today, tomorrow and forever more and may "Thy will be done on earth as it is in heaven." (Luke 11:2)

October 6-2012
Osoyoos, B.C.
Rev. E. Stefaniuk

CPSIA information can be obtained at www.ICGtesting.com
Printed in the USA
BVOW081858070313

314994BV00001B/53/P